863035

The Practical
Motorcaravanner

The Practical Motorcaravanner

John Hunt

863035 /496.79

DAVID & CHARLES
Newton Abbot   London   North Pomfret (Vt)

British Library Cataloguing in Publication Data

Hunt, John
    The practical motorcaravanner
    1. Campers and coaches, Truck
    I. Title
    796.7'9   TL298

ISBN 0–7153–8428–7

Filmset by Latimer Trend & Company Ltd, Plymouth
and printed in Great Britain
by Butler & Tanner Limited, Frome and London
for David & Charles (Publishers) Limited
Brunel House   Newton Abbot   Devon

Published in the United States of America
by David & Charles Inc
North Pomfret   Vermont 05053   USA

Contents

Acknowledgements

To the thousands of motorcaravanners who have contributed to this book by their letters and articles sent to me as Editor of *Motorcaravan + Motorhome Monthly*.

To Jack Wildbore, publisher of *MMM*, who launched the magazine and kept it going through the early years of financial strain.

To my wife and secretary, Audrey, without whose constant help, encouragement and memory jogging the book would never have been finished.

To the late Henry Myhill, author and ardent motorcaravanner, who inspired so many with accounts of his journeys and sojourns in Europe and North Africa.

Introduction

The easy way to write a book about motorcaravans is to rehash sales brochures in different words. But this book is more about motorcaravanning than motorcaravans. Readers will not find detailed descriptions of current models, although there are plenty of illustrations which classify the variations on the home-on-four-wheels theme. The intention is to help readers to select the types of motorcaravans best suited to their own particular circumstances and to use them to the fullest possible advantage, all the year round.

For detailed reviews of latest models, new and secondhand prices, travel articles, letters about all aspects, advice on modifications and DIY, motorcaravanners are recommended to subscribe to a specialist magazine.

This book will, I hope, point you in the right direction and help you to reach the goal of happy motorcaravanning.

1
Why motorcaravanning?

Your interest in motorcaravanning may go only as far as wondering what makes more and more apparently sane men and women drive around in lumbering, uncomfortable, thirsty, slow and noisy delivery vans with windows. A motorcar is surely more comfortable and thrifty, faster and quieter? You may, on the other hand, have more than a passing curiosity about these vehicles. It could be that you have considered hiring one for holidays (being so much easier to handle than a car plus trailer caravan), but have not yet taken the plunge. Or, perhaps, you are a real camper (canvas variety) and would now relish a little more comfort and a lot less work when setting up your temporary home. You could, of course, be a trailer caravanner — or a potential trailer caravanner with nowhere to park the caravan — most homes do not yet have space for a caravan or boat.

It is likely, however, that as you have picked up this book, you are already a motorcaravanner or seriously thinking about it. You might even know it all, and just be skipping through these pages to discover something you do not agree with. There will be plenty, because motorcaravanners are individualists. There is something for everyone, for this book is a summary of the experiences of hundreds of motorcaravanners — thousands, probably — with whom I have talked or corresponded over the last twenty-three years during which I have been a motorcaravanning editor.

There was a time when my wife and I thought that driving a motorcaravan was an inferior sort of motoring, something we had to put up with for the undoubted advantages of cheap family holidays. If we had been able to afford it, we would have run a car and kept the motorcaravan for weekends and holidays. In those days, commercial vans really were commercial, with no attempt from their manufacturers to cater for creature comforts. Germany led the way, with the classless, all purpose Volkswagen bus. British vans were not all that bad and they were a lot cheaper. We began to learn of the many advantages from the driver's and passenger's angle.

For one thing, it is wonderful being so high. There is much

more to see, not only on the road ahead, but all around. It is more relaxing than concentrating all one's attention on the strip of road in front. An hour—or a day—behind the wheel of a motorcaravan leaves both driver and passengers less fatigued than in a low-slung motorcar. And, if the ground between A and B has not been covered quite so quickly, it has been a lot more pleasurable. There has been more to observe and appreciate.

How often have your children grizzled, 'Are we nearly there?' We grew accustomed to such plaintive cries from the back of the car five minutes after starting a journey, repeated at regular intervals throughout the run. And in the very early days, what a worry were bottles and potties. Whereas, with disposable nappies and insulated feeding bottles, things are a lot easier for modern mothers, there are undoubted advantages in having the use of a gas ring when it is needed and in being able to wash the hands after changing even a super-absorbent cellulose nappy.

The presence at all times of what can be called the essential life-support systems is one of the great joys of motorcaravanning. No matter what the weather, there is the wherewithal for relaxation and sustenance whenever needed, at any time of the day or night. It is invaluable when there are children.

Driver fatigue, so often the cause of accidents, is avoidable. In a motorcaravan, you can stop and make a quick cup of strong tea or coffee. No need to search hopelessly for a café when only the pubs are open. And how often have long-distance motorists driven on and on, looking for somewhere to satisfy the inner man, or for a stopping place where all the needs of nature can be satisfied? A properly equipped motorcaravan will have them all on board. If all else fails, there is even a bed.

How frequently must travellers caught in a snow drift have longed for a few home comforts? Even a partially buried motorcaravan will continue to function as a life-support module. The gas will still work, provided it is propane and not butane (but attention must be given to providing adequate ventilation, for a gas flame is as big a consumer of oxygen as a human being). My family well remembers setting out from northern Scotland to motor south, just after Christmas. We had listened avidly to weather forecasts and decided there was no undue danger. But, an hour after we had started, snow fell and the motor began to stutter. I put it down to dampness penetrating the ignition, and conjectured that the best course was to keep motoring and not allow revs to drop too low. Passing through an isolated little town, the beast gave a final shudder and died.

As luck would have it, we had noticed a small garage a few hundred yards back. Donning wellies and anorak (always aboard a fully equipped motorcaravan) I slithered the intervening distance. The helpful Scots owner immediately turned out to tow us in. Our big coachbuilt was too high to be squeezed into the little repair shop but we managed to push the bonnet under cover. A broken distributor cap was soon diagnosed. The garage held a Leyland franchise and we were in a Bedford, but our luck was in that day. There just happened to be one odd cap in stock, and it fitted. We celebrated by brewing fresh coffee for the garage man, his staff of one and ourselves, then continued our drive through snow which gradually turned to slush.

At no time were we unduly worried. As with all our motorcaravans, big or small, we were equipped with all the necessities for living for at least a couple of days. We could have wintered, if not comfortably, at least in safety overnight or until succour came from one of the efficient highland rescue services. In the event, we reached Gretna Green soon after dark and booked in at the little motel. (Just because you are a motorcaravanner, you do not have to spend every night in the thing. A motorcaravan, unlike a car–plus–trailer caravan combination, can be used purely as a car when it so pleases the owners.)

The motorcaravan, however, is much more than a mobile cooking, eating, sitting and sleeping room. It is more, even, than an ever-present refuge in time of trouble. It can be a removal van or a dustcart to take rubbish to the tip. It is an ever-available spare bedroom. It can be a minibus, for taking your own and neighbours' children to school or on outings to the seaside. Children love it and are fascinated by all the gadgets, which must be demonstrated time after time. A couple of motorcaravans can transport a school football team and provide the necessary backup facilities and sustenance. A word of warning here. Do not accept payment, because this is illegal unless you hold a taxi or public service vehicle operator's licence. If you are offered money to pay for the petrol, it is as well to consult your insurance company or broker before accepting. Though many policies allow a driver to be reimbursed for reasonable out of pocket travelling expenses,

11

Many motorcaravans can be adapted for wheelchairs. This CI Travelhome was equipped with twin rear doors and tail lift by Corvesgate Coachcraft

the dividing line between social-domestic-pleasure and business use can be difficult to distinguish from the small print of a policy. If you do transport large numbers of people, the insurance company should be informed, whether or not expenses are shared.

Your motorcaravan can give the aged a new lease of life. They can sit up, with ample leg room, even walk to their seats (or be helped) rather than having to be shoehorned in, with the inevitable difficulties of bending arthritic joints. And when they are installed in their seats, they can see much more of the world outside.

Those who have tried motorcaravanning with the handicapped have found it to be almost the ideal form of travel and recreation. I have heard from a lot of disabled drivers who are motorcaravanners, that a popular delivery van (on which all motorcaravans are based, with the exception of some huge American rigs) is as easy to adapt as any car. Automatic transmission, for instance, is available on all but some of the tiny Japanese vans and power steering is not as rare as it was. A platform to take a wheelchair and occupant can be fitted to rear or side doors and be raised and lowered electrically. The non-driving disabled person can, if more comfortable, travel within the vehicle in the wheelchair, securely fastened of course. And, in suitable vehicles, toilet facilities are on board and immediately available. Though many of the production-line motorcaravans have not been designed with the handicapped in mind, adaptation to their special needs is a fairly simple matter and there are firms specialising in the work.

Certainly, a motorcaravan will initially cost a little more than the equivalent standard-production motorcar. (Light delivery vans usually share engines and other components with cars from the same manufacturer.) But the customer is getting a lot more for his money in the way of installed equipment. Some motorcaravanners are even beginning to complain that their vehicles have become too luxurious and too well fitted. They yearn for the days of simple vans with few concessions to home comforts—but they are in the minority.

It is not only in fixtures and fittings that the motorcaravan scores over a car. It is altogether a more rugged vehicle, with a de-tuned engine rather than a highly stressed one from which the maximum of power must be squeezed. It has been built for a hard working life, for the majority of commercial operators will opt for a van which can be expected to give long and trustworthy service, with the minimum of time off the road. Commercial vehicles are expected to run for 100,000 miles or more with only routine servicing and, when overhaul or repairs are needed, their owners want a fast turn-round with instant availability of the more common spare parts. This is not to say that these vehicles are never subject to the usual hiccups and lack of availability of spares. Delays do occur, of course, but the owner is unlikely to find his transport off the road for months because of the lack of, for instance, a special rear lamp cluster peculiar to that one model. The vehicles on which motorcaravans are based do not change in appearance from year to year according to the dictates of fashion.

The motorcaravan is unlikely to cost more for routine service jobs than the car to which it is related. Sometimes the reverse is the case. Expecting to pay some £90 for a full service on my last motorcaravan, which was the price displayed for its related car, I was delighted to be presented with a bill for £10 less. 'Didn't take so long,' said the foreman, 'It's all more accessible.'

There was another pleasant surprise when I changed from a run-of-the-mill car to a motorcaravan of larger engine capacity. A refund arrived from the insurance company because the new vehicle slotted into a lower group. The car was advertised for its ability to be first away in the traffic-light grand prix and was reputed to be capable of the 'ton up'. Nobody, least of all the insurance company, would expect such claims to be made for a motorcaravan, so we moved at a stroke from insurance group 5 to group 2; this was in spite of the fact that the motorcaravan cost rather more to buy and had much more in the way of furniture and effects within its body shell.

When the time eventually came to sell the motorcaravan, depreciation was less of a shock than it had been with the car. The latter had halved in value in less than two years, whereas, after a similar interval, the motorcaravan actually fetched more than I gave for it, though I must confess to a few alterations to the interior. (In common with many others, I probably spend more time in the motorcaravan when it is at home than in travelling and camping.)

The comparatively low rate of depreciation of most standard motorcaravans is an agreeable surprise. The market for five- or six-year-old cars is limited, on the whole, because at that age they are beginning to be called bangers. A five-year-old motorcaravan that has been treasured will be worth a higher proportion of its initial cost and, in favourable circumstances, could equal or exceed it. I am told that the book price of one particular and popular model is exactly the same as when it was new fifteen years ago. If you try to buy one from a dealer, you will be asked up to £1,000 more than that for a good privately bought specimen.

When I changed from the aforementioned car to the motorcaravan, I had expected to spend a lot more on petrol. The initial shock was not too bad, from a four star 28mpg on the car to a two star 25mpg with the much heavier motorcaravan. Admittedly, the small difference was mainly due to the fact that the larger vehicle was slower off the mark and neither it nor its occupants felt the need to demonstrate superiority by overtaking whatever happened to be in front.

The ground did not slip away beneath the wheels quite so

rapidly but we found yet again (this was not our first motorca-ravan) that a given run of, say, 200 miles over varied roads took no longer, and we arrived more relaxed. A fast car will, naturally, return a faster journey time if most of the run is on motorways, although much of that difference is diminishing for law-abiding motorists. The newer breeds of base vehicles for motorcaravans will cruise at the legal maximum if you want them to but you will enjoy the motoring more on main and secondary roads where, because you are sitting high, there is more to see.

Motorcaravanning should not be confused with any other form of leisure activity. Towing a trailer caravan (or trailer tent) may seem comparable in that you have got your home with you. The same could be said of a tent in the boot or on the roof rack. The similarity ends there. What is the first thing you do with trailer or tent? Find somewhere to park or pitch it, of course. Then, having taken your time getting installed, you can use the unencumbered/uncluttered car for trips out. This aspect will be examined more fully in Chapter 3.

Most caravanners find a pitch, put the brake on and get out the kettle and teapot, because they are in business straight away. And, when they go out for a day, the motorcaravan, with all its life-support systems, goes with them. It is entirely up to them as to whether they go on to pastures new or return to last night's stand. The point is, they do not have to return to pick up the caravan or tent. With a motorcaravan, you can travel further and record less mileage because you are not compelled to retrace your steps back to site.

Sometimes, when inspecting a showroom or salesground, my wife and I have come across a trailer caravan which offered superior appointments or had a better layout than our motorca-ravan. Occasionally we have seen a folder or trailer tent which could be stored unobtrusively in our little garage (where the motorcaravan will not fit). More than once we have been tempted into an impulse buy, which we have later regretted, and paid dearly for the experience. So nobody can say that we have never tried the alternatives. For reasons which I hope will become obvious to all who read this book, we are now convinced that motorcaravanning is best.

2
Development of the motorcaravan

There have been motorcaravans since there were cars and commercial vehicles. During World War I, my father drove an ice lorry in Mesopotamia, my mother drove an ambulance in Britain, and both could spend a more or less comfortable night in their vehicles. I spent a considerable time in the following war driving a 4 × 4 Bedford towing a gun. I equipped it surreptitiously with basic life-support systems (petrol stove, tin of soup or beans, blanket) and spent much more comfortable nights on manoeuvres than the rest of the gun crew. The army spawned another rather more famous and innovative motorcaravanner — Monty himself.

It took the early Martin Walter Dormobiles, at the 1958 Motor Show, to open my eyes to motorcaravans and both my wife and myself wish now that we had stretched our resources to the limit and taken out a mortgage on one. But the price was £700 and being a dedicated DIY addict, I decided I could do better.

Commercial light vans then available were Austin-Morris 152/J2, Bedford CA, Ford Thames, Standard Atlas and Volkswagen. (There must have been a Commer/Karrier but memory fails.) The Austin-Morris was too big, a salesman told me that Bedfords rolled over on corners, Fords were on strike and the VW was expensive. So we ended up with a disastrous Standard Atlas — more about this and other mistakes in the DIY Chapter 6.

The early Dormobile caravans gave a generic term to the market. Their contemporaries, Volkswagen-based and made by the Devon firm of J. P. White & Co, were called Caravettes — another trade name which has passed into the language. Nobody has yet come up with a better portmanteau term than Dormobile or Caravette but there have been several worthy failures, like Moto-Caravan. This was another VW conversion, by a naturalised German named Peter Pitt. Pitt claimed, with some justification, to have invented the modern motorcaravan but he died in comparative obscurity some time after his organisation had been taken over by another manufacturer.

One of the earliest Dormobiles, c 1959. The tents emphasise the camping background of the owners. Contrast the rising roof with the modern version on page 31

So, basically, there were two types of motorcaravan conversions of popular light vans in the late fifties and early sixties. All genuine Dormobiles were at first based upon the Bedford CA van. Martin Walter Ltd of Folkestone had, in fact, been using the CA for a sort of sleeping van some time earlier, having developed it from the successful utility (or Tilly) runabouts of war years. Very early Dormobiles were passenger carriers, with seats which could be made into longitudinal benches for sleeping. Before long a rudimentary cooking stove was incorporated, then a bowl for washing up, but it is safe to say that the real motorcaravan came when someone at Martin Walters cut a hole in the roof and fitted a hinged glass–fibre top, with sidewalls of flexible plastic. Motorcaravanners were at last able to stand up to dress or undress.

The rising roof (British Standards Institution prefer that term to 'elevating') rapidly grew in size until virtually the whole top section of the original van was removed. This meant that the glass-fibre top enveloped the van from gutter to gutter. The cab roof was never, in those days, cut away for fear of weakening the whole structure. At first an ordinary roof rack was supplied as an optional

17

extra for the front part but it was not long before the manufacturers made a neat glass-fibre rack to mate with the rising part of
the roof. The Bedford CA van had become a vehicle with eye
appeal and some of the models produced in the sixties are now
prized by collectors. They are still, arguably, some of the best
looking motorcaravans ever produced. They were fairly low and
sleek, with a vestigial bonnet at the front which seemed to make
car drivers happy. They certainly appealed to the car driving
journalists who road tested them. They liked the driving position,
with feet well out in front and the steering wheel angled as on a car
instead of nearly flat as in a bus.

Inside, the Dormobile set the trend which is still popular today
on van conversions: front seats which, when fully reclined,
matched with rear seats, backs similarly reclined, to make a pair of
longitudinal beds. So there were four forward-facing seats for
travelling. If only the rear seats had their backrests reclined, there
were two little benches on which four people could sit facing a
table in the centre gangway. There was room at the rear for a
built-in gas cooker, sink and storage units. A wardrobe was
compulsory. If there was not a wardrobe and certain other
equipment specified by Her Majesty's Inspectors of Customs and
Excise, the owner had to pay purchase tax, for the vehicle was
considered to be a car, which was taxable, rather than a caravan,
which was not.

Another converter whose products were admired in the early
days was Kenex of Dover. A few of its converted Bedford CAs
survive and are recognizable by the louvred windows in the van's
rear doors and a roof which rises vertically, having striped plastic
walls on all four sides. Kenex was taken over by its neighbour at
Folkestone, Martin Walter, who later became Dormobile Ltd but
is now itself regrettably, out of the motorcaravan scene.

Along with the Bedford CA, other delivery vans were being
made into motorcaravans by enterprising manufacturers all over
the country, for those early sixties were the age of expansion. The
Austin 152 (or Morris J2 with a slightly different front end, for
these were the days of badge engineering when virtually identical
models were given different names) became popular for the very
reason I had, in my DIY efforts, rejected it as being too big. It was
just over 6ft (1.8m) wide internally. This opened up a whole new
field of interior design, for a bed could be sited crossways.

There was soon a Dormobile Austin-Morris. There was a transverse bulkhead which converters were afraid (or forbidden) to remove. So Dormobile, like most others, left the cab with the spartan trim and seats supplied by the manufacturers and installed its own layout in the 9 × 6ft (2.7 × 1.8m) van interior. Because of the van's extra width, the Dormobile roof, which now spanned the whole top as a matter of course, rose higher when pushed up on its hinges. The proud boast was that interior headroom was in excess of 9ft (2.7m). All very well, but the beds would only accommodate sleepers up to 6ft (1.8m) in height.

An early starter with the Austin-Morris was Car Campers Ltd. It had the ingenious idea of putting a 4 × 6ft (1.2 × 1.8m) mattress on the floor and covering it with a false floor, on which were mounted a folding dining table and folding settees. At bed time, instead of shuffling with reclining seat backs and cushions, the only chore facing caravanners was to fold down the table and settees, fold up the floor, and there was revealed a ready-made double bed.

Car Camper interior from the early sixties. The ready-made double bed is hidden beneath the platform

It did not really catch on as a permanent feature. It seems that caravanners did not like sleeping on the floor and Car Campers gradually switched over to what has since become the second conventional layout of twin, inward-facing settees behind the cab, with a table which can be lowered to bridge the gap between them. Moving cushions around makes a transverse bed.

At about the same time, a small firm in the Cotswolds began producing entirely conventional motorcaravans on the Austin-Morris with the twin-settees-behind-cab layout which was gradually becoming so popular. But Auto-Sleepers had a different roof, raised on a parallelogramming principle, and constructed of entirely solid material. It gave better insulation and freedom from flapping fabric sidewalls. Auto-Sleepers began slowly in the sixties, making a reputation for well constructed and nicely finished cabinet work from the Cotswold craftsmen. Auto-Sleepers still produces the same basic design, which later incorporated rear seats that could be made to face forwards for travelling. The quality of construction and finish which has been maintained over the years is still the standard by which other conversions are measured. This firm has lately launched other layouts on a variety of vehicles, but all remain instantly recognisable as Auto-Sleepers.

There were further varied attempts to produce rising roofs with rigid walls, but the only other firm who is still very much in production is the motorcaravan branch of the giant Caravans International, now called Autohomes (UK). It began conversions with the Bluebird Wanderer (Bluebird was a branch of Caravans International). But the first Bluebird motorcaravan was a different kettle of fish and leads us to an entirely different type of motorcaravan.

Coachbuilts, or motorhomes as they tend to be called, are based on a cab and chassis supplied by the motor manufacturer. They were obviously inspired by special high-capacity bodies which extended over the cab and were called Lutons (probably from the town). The commercial Luton-type body was too high and ugly for motorcaravan customers and a special one was built, more compact and with some attempt at styling. Trailer-caravan influence was prominent in both external appearance and interior layout and Bluebird, who had made a name building cheap but adequate and deservedly popular trailer caravans, lent its name to

Luxury from 1962. Coachbuilt Paralanian on Austin 152 chassis

the Bluebird Highwayman. It remained for years the cheapest coachbuilt motorhome. I have never been quite sure why a mass-produced trailer-caravan body could not have been mounted on a chassis-cab, so cutting costs. Manufacturers say it would just fall to pieces. So motorhomes have always had purpose-built bodies, produced in fairly small quantities — and consequently compara-tively expensive.

Nevertheless, the first Highwaymen in the early sixties were sold at a little under £900 and, considering the extra space they gave within the body, were good value. Base vehicles were initially Austin-Morris, rather underpowered by today's standards with the 1489cc engine. The Commer Highwayman came later. Alongside the Highwayman, and on the same base vehicle because none other was available, ran the far superior Paralanian, unashamedly a coachbuilt for two people and, at £1,250, appealing mainly to the well-heeled retired couple.

One or two other motorhomes made their appearance before

the seventies, some to stay, others to fade almost as soon as they had had the wraps removed. Interior appointments were gradually improved, too, as was body insulation, to tempt owners to go motorcaravanning throughout the year. Probably the biggest single step was the inclusion of what manufacturers insist upon calling the toilet room. In fact they usually mean a small compartment or large cupboard in which a chemical closet can be sited and used. Nowadays, several motorhomes are equipped with rooms in which one can perform a complete toilet, including indulgence in the luxury of a bath or shower.

For a long time the space over the cab on coachbuilt motorhomes formed a useful storage compartment. It was CI Autohomes (now Autohomes UK) who introduced into Britain an idea which was pioneered by the Americans in their much larger motorhomes—the now ubiquitous overcab bed. Whether you want it or not, it is there, an asset for families, when children (who usually love it) can be put to bed out of the way. Those whose families have grown up and left home are not so sure. Few caravanning couples need all that space for storage and the increased frontal area must adversely affect fuel consumption. Some accept it as a bonus and make use of what they are forced to have, sleeping upstairs and leaving the table downstairs set for breakfast.

The sixties and early seventies brought some brilliant ideas which failed for lack of exploitation, drive, cash or from pure bad luck. Others were ridiculous and doomed to obscurity. The reader may decide into which category the following few examples fall.

A lot of fuss was made in the early eighties by a manufacturer who produced an electrically raised roof on his conversions. It was even called innovative, which it certainly was not. Airborne offered it, first as standard then as an extra, on roofs twenty years previously—and Airborne roofs were solid structures, with no flapping canvas-type material. Most Airbornes were on Ford Thames vans no longer than the related Consul.

A couple of bright Yorkshiremen produced the Nomad on the Austin-Morris. This had a roof which was wound up with a handle, working on the lazy-tongs principle, with a cable concealed in the rain channel to operate the lazy-tongs. Again, electric operation was an extra—they replaced the handle with a starter motor and automatic switch for reversing polarity.

1960s conversion of Morris J2 van, with ventilated rising roof, by Canterbury—a rare photograph

Ford Thames Airborne conversion, with upturned boat providing standing height within

Canterbury Industrial Products (who began as Canterbury Sidecars) had a vertically rising roof with canvas sidewalls all round. The turn of a button released a frame holding the sidewalls, increasing ventilation dramatically and allowing standing occupants of the vehicle a grandstand view of what was around.

Auto-Sleepers arranged for the rigid sidewalls of the roof to be folded inwards, a little or a lot, to increase ventilation or provide a grandstand view. This one, fortunately, is still very much with us.

Airborne made one of the first permanent high-top motorcaravan conversions. The van's roof was cut off in the usual way, but instead of fitting a rising roof, Airborne installed what looked like an upturned glass-fibre boat—not surprising, because it was a boat!

On the same nautical theme, Caraboot took a standard Mini van. It then built a caravan shell, with a road wheel at each side, and omitted the front wall. For travelling, the caravan shell fitted closely around the Mini's body, which made a little van into a six wheeler. On site, the caravan was unhooked and the van driven

The extraordinary Caraboot, all based upon a BLMC Mini van

Wildgoose on Mini. Body sides extend vertically to provide standing room

forwards five or six feet, which operation provided a living space at least twice as long as the vehicle. On top, an upturned glass-fibre boat was carried.

Wildgoose of Worthing also started with a Mini van. It hacksawed off the entire rear end and threw it away, retaining only a few essential parts such as wheels and suspension units. A double-walled caravan body was built, with a gap between the walls, rather wider and longer than the part discarded. It had a floor but no roof. The wheels were bolted on to this and the lot was attached to the van's front end, making a nice little motorised caravan with cavity walls but without a roof. So Wildgoose built another caravan body, with a roof and single-thickness walls, but with no floor. The caravan body without floor fitted exactly over and into the motorised caravan with no roof. With a drum and cable added, it was possible to raise and lower the roof and the attached sidewalls. Electric operation was an extra. It may sound crude but it really worked and provided what was probably the first 40mpg coachbuilt motorcaravan. I suppose the vast amount of work entailed meant that the selling price was disproportionately high, though Wildgoose tried to cut the cost by fitting a more ordinary rising roof in place of the VEB (vertically extending body). Unfortunately, Wildgoose was not with us for long. That one deserved to succeed and it must have been well

25

made. Until at least ten years after the Wildgoose had flown, I passed almost daily a survivor. Unfortunately, he was always going in the other direction, otherwise I would have chased him for a chat.

In spite of what trailer-caravan manufacturers recommended (ie don't) one enterprising individual removed some caravans from their chassis, cut away the lower part of the front end and slid it over a standard chassis-cab. It looked as though a motorist had braked rather too hard when towing his caravan. Unfortunately, the manufacturer was not granted approval by either chassis or caravan manufacturers and, on the model a disappointed customer asked me to inspect, he had neglected the formality of fitting safety glass to the caravan's windows, so it could not be driven legally on any public road. I do not think many of these were produced, which disappointed me because I would like to know whether, in fact, the trailer-caravan body would stand mounting on a four-wheeled chassis. It has been done on a Mercedes by Carlight, but Carlights are rather special caravans.

The VW buffs will now be wondering whether I have forgotten the ubiquitous Volkswagen. But the faithful old bus deserves a section to itself.

The split-windscreen Volkswagen Kombi or Minibus was the basis of many early, rudimentary conversions, usually without rising roofs. They were more like camping cars, for life was a trifle cramped inside if the doors could not be opened, and cooking and washing chores had to be performed outside. Most early VWs had the gas cooker mounted on one of the hinged doors. The advent of the sliding door put a stop to that but old habits die hard and there were some ingenious dual-height cookers, located just inside the door opening, which could be used inside or out.

Rising roofs grew in popularity and spread to the Volks. The vehicle manufacturers insisted upon special chassis strengthening plates if an aperture was to be cut in the van's roof. All this, plus import costs, ensured that the VW remained at the top of the price bracket. By the time the new VW transporter was introduced in the late seventies, the rising roof had become an almost universal fitting and the kitchen unit was transferred to the offside on nearly all conversions, often running the full length of the body and providing a great deal of storage space. The VW camping car had become a motorcaravan.

This early Calthorpe VW has a door-mounted cooker that can be used outside

Forgive my boast; I think I invented the first really small motorcaravan. It was based on the old-type Ford Escort 100E, 1100cc van and is described briefly in the DIY Chapter 6. It was exhibited on the Motor Caravanners' Club's stand at a COLEX (Camping & Outdoor Life) show in London in 1963.

A year or so later, I was invited to road test Martin Walter's first Roma motorcaravan conversion of the little HA van. I was glad but not flattered, because it was nothing like mine. The Dormobile had reclining front seats which mated with rear seats to form a double bed and there was the option of a child's bunk in the rising roof. The Roma was followed by a trickle of similar conversions of the Ford Escort, Austin $\frac{1}{2}$ ton and later BL Marina vans. It has been an interesting sideline but production figures have never been startling.

High-top conversions of panel vans have not been big sellers either, although a prominent manufacturer informs me that they are likely to be the motorcaravan of the future. The first one I remember was called a Cotswold, based on the then increasingly popular Austin-Morris 152/J2. It gave permanent headroom and little else, but they have progressed since early days and will be dealt with more fully in the next chapter.

Surprisingly, dismountables (preferable to the more popular 'demountables' by BSI) came late on the scene. Commercial body

27

builders Walkers of Watford saw the possibility. A business man, possibly a small builder, would buy a truck for daily use and plonk a caravan body upon it for holidays. Others tried the same idea but, although Walkers continues to produce dismountable caravans, the idea has never meant big business.

In the late seventies, an enterprising builder of glass-fibre kit cars invented a small, two-berth dismountable body for little Japanese trucks. After some production hiccups, the Romahome is now establishing a place in the market. It is the cheapest motorcaravan available, undercutting its nearest rival by £1,000 or more (in 1983). A similar product, made by the same firm and called Hitch Hiker, allows owners of standard hatchback cars to carry a little folding caravan on the sloping rear end.

Imported models from America were made available by the pioneer dealer, Wilsons, in the sixties, after Leslie Wilson had had one or two attempts at building his own 3 ton luxury motorhomes. (Wilson, the first dealer to stock motorcaravans in quantity, was affectionately known as Mr Motorcaravan. He organised the first motorcaravan rally at Woburn Abbey and ran the first test days at Brands Hatch motor racing circuit, the forerunner of the big National Motorcaravan Fair.)

Nowadays, American imports are supplemented by a few from Germany. Other European countries, having like Germany caught the motorcaravanning bug from Britain, are slow to jump upon the bandwagon. Meanwhile, this country continues to export motorcaravans in small quantities but the industry is not helped by a punitive tax system which stifles the home market.

The sixties and early seventies saw an expanding industry. Thanks to the purchase-tax concessions, motorcaravans were a really good buy. The crunch came in 1973, when value added tax replaced purchase tax and, overnight, motorcaravan manufacturers found themselves saddled, not only with VAT, but with a 10 per cent car tax as well. Increased prices ensured that home demand fell away, followed inevitably by reduced exports. The age of innovation came to a stop and, as has so often happened in other spheres, foreign markets introduced their own models.

The little industry is still reeling under the blow but there are signs, at last, of some sort of recovery and the established names who have weathered a troubled decade are beginning to have the courage to experiment again with some interesting developments.

3
Which motorcaravan?

The choice is wide and thoroughly confusing to newcomers. I receive many letters from potential motorcaravanners who are bewildered, seeking suggestions for what they should buy. Unless they know fairly definitely what is expected of the motorcaravan, it is difficult to give specific advice because motorcaravanning is such an individual occupation. It is an important choice, calling for a substantial outlay second only to that of the home. This is a decision that must not be rushed and it is worth spending a bit of time and money to ensure that the vehicle eventually chosen will not be a disaster.

There are scores of different motorcaravans produced by the established converters who tend to stay in business. Add to those the hundreds which are made by smaller firms, who tend to come and go, and there should be something for everybody. Most practising caravanners, with the exception of some who have designed their own from the wheels up, will say that the ideal motorcaravan will never be produced. The majority of motorcaravans consist of two distinct parts: base vehicle and caravan accommodation, amalgamated in varying degrees. Some have entirely separate driving compartments, whilst others use the front seats as an integral part of the living area. With a few exceptions (some in the USA and one in Germany), nobody produces a vehicle designed specifically to become a motorcaravan or motorhome. So the choice of base vehicles is severely limited. For this reason, I am dealing with the selection of a motorcaravan first. It is the more important consideration. The vehicles will be discussed in the next chapter. See pages 45–55 for diagrams of different caravan layouts.

So, how do you decide which motorcaravan will suit your particular circumstances? Ask yourself and family these questions:

Is it to be the only car?

Will it be used mainly for holidays?

Do you propose motorcaravanning in winter?

Must it go into a garage?

How many people will use it?

Do you want to tow a trailer?
Do you want single beds?
Do you want a separate room for children?
Do you require a complete motorcaravan?
What other considerations are there?

Before expanding on these points, newcomers will need to be conversant with the various types of motorcaravans.

Conversions of light delivery vans, often called panel vans, are the commonest, occasionally referred to erroneously as 'Caravettes', 'Dormobiles' or 'Auto-Sleepers' (these are trade names). Essentially, they are ordinary vans with windows cut in the sides. There is usually a rising roof or high top, fitted after removing most of the steel roof.

Coachbuilts start with a cab and chassis from the vehicle manufacturer on which a body is built. Most builders employ a conventional coachbuilding technique, which consists of a framework of wood or metal clad inside and out with various sheet materials. Variations include pre-formed sandwich panels which are, to put it simply, fastened together to form a box. Glass fibre (glass reinforced plastic or GRP) is sometimes used for roof panels or even the whole body. Coachbuilts are often referred to as motorhomes.

Class A motorhomes start with wheels and chassis. The coachbuilder adds the body, which includes the driving compartment. The latter therefore becomes part of the living accommodation. The idea was initiated, like so many others, in the USA and has now spread to several European countries but Britain has been slow to adopt it.

Dismountables (or demountables) have a coachbuilt body on a flatbed or pickup truck. The body can be taken off and used rather like a sited trailer caravan, leaving the base vehicle free for travelling or business activities.

Fifth wheelers or semi-trailers are, again, an American idea and occasionally available in Britain secondhand. They are similar to articulated commercial vehicles, except that the load area has become a caravan. Like dismountables, they can be left on site whilst the tractor unit (often a pickup truck) is used for travelling.

Having classified motorcaravans, we can return to selecting the best type for your circumstances.

A modern VW conversion—the Moonraker by Devon

Sherpa Leisure motorcaravan by Auto-Sleepers, first introduced at the Motor Show, 1982

Luxury high-top conversion of Ford Transit van by Pampas

The only car?

If it is the only car you will need something fairly compact and not over-thirsty on fuel. It should not be too big to slot into a parking-meter bay or a supermarket car park, though it is unlikely that you will be able to take advantage of multi-storey garages. This probably points to a panel-van conversion, which is seldom much longer than an estate car, though it will be a little wider and a lot higher. The choice here is enormous unless you happen to want a 'complete' motorcaravan, with a toilet compartment. There are very few of these but I suspect that they will grow in popularity over the next few years. You will have the choice of a high-top or rising-roof model. The permanent high top adds little, if anything, to fuel consumption and offers better insulation (though there are exceptions) and more storage space. Some people object to the overall vehicle height of 8ft (2.4m) or more and choose a conversion with a rising roof, which is lowered for travelling.

There are many types of rising roofs but only two subdivisions: walls that are rigid or walls of a waterproof, flexible material — usually a plastic. The top, or cap, is always rigid and almost invariably of GRP. Rigid sides allow better insulation and, because windows or openable panels are often incorporated, more ventilation options. Flexible walls make for simplicity of erection, often just a gentle heave upwards, and allow the designer the opportunity to push the walls outwards and provide yet more space inside. There are many variations on the two themes. At least one all-rigid roof extends sideways as well as upwards and some with flexible sides cover the whole length of the vehicle, allowing occupants to walk into the cab, which then becomes part of the living area. The extra height and space gained with a rising roof or high top is usually made to accommodate extra beds, either stretcher bunks or beds with solid bases and mattresses.

Mainly for holidays?

If the motorcaravan is to fulfil only one of its many possible functions, the chances are that it will be a recreational vehicle (RV). In that case, there is probably another car in the family which is used for shopping and plain travelling and the size of the motorcaravan will become less critical. In this case, go for the largest you think you can manage.

In the showroom, you may be tempted into believing that small is beautiful, and for day-to-day use, where parkability is important, it is. But take that compact little package away from home for a fortnight or more and live in it full time: you will wish you could push the walls out and will long to sit, for a change, in an undisciplined sprawl with arms akimbo and legs stretched. Space is yet more important with a family but even a couple need at

GRP monocoque construction of this Auto-Sleeper on Bedford gives flowing lines

A compact A-class from Germany—the Mercedes Tabbert

times to be able to move around independently of each other. My wife and I, with family off our hands, imagined we could cope in our compact but complete little high-top conversion. We managed, but, both being rather untidy and undisciplined, did not enjoy the experience. An extended road test of a coachbuilt opened our eyes. It was delightful to be able to relax, legs up or on the floor at will, and actually have room to walk past each other.

In consistently fine weather, space is not so important. A few hours or days of rain bring home the lesson. A later chapter will deal with ways of extending the living accommodation of a small vehicle but I do not think you will ever regret buying the biggest you can afford to run and are happy to drive.

Camping in winter?

This should be qualified by 'in temperate climates'. If you are one of the lucky ones able to chase the winter sun (see Chapter 10) almost any motorcaravan will be suitable. But in the northern parts of the continental land mass and its nearby islands, you will need heat and enough insulation to prevent this expensive form of energy warming the atmosphere outside rather than the motorcaravan's occupants.

In this respect, oddly enough, big becomes beautiful. My wife and I have never been really cosy in a very small motorcaravan. Once I had finished playing with it, eliminating all cold surfaces with carpet and double glazing, the Sherpa with high top was about the smallest in which we have felt snug. It had the expensive German Eberspächer blown-air heating system which drew its fuel from the petrol tank — more about that in Chapter 7. The point is, there must be room for a heater to be installed, if one is not already supplied. To supplement the heater, there must be adequate ventilation and good insulation. Generally speaking, coachbuilts are better insulated than van conversions but there is a lot the DIY man can do to improve the latter (see Chapter 7).

Must it go into a garage?

This, for many dwellers in town and suburban houses, will impose tremendous limitations. Most domestic garages have doors which are about 6ft 6in (2m) high, some as low as 6ft (1.8m). Very few motorcaravans are less than 7ft (2.1m) high, high tops exceed that by 1ft (30cm) or so and coachbuilts are 9ft (2.7m) plus. If you can park the vehicle in your drive or roadway, it is not going to suffer from the weather, more likely it will benefit by the free circulation of air. Unventilated or poorly ventilated garages encourage condensation which will lead to problems with rust. A car port, open at the ends, is excellent, for healthy breezes can blow through. If you live in an area subject to heavy industrial pollution, vandalism or salt spray from the sea, a closed garage could be the lesser of the two evils. Then you will need to shop around with a tape measure (do not trust the figures in the brochure). An average 16 × 8ft (4.9 × 2.4m) garage with 6ft 6in (2m) doors means you will be looking at rising-roof conversions of the miniature vans, most popular of which is the Fiat 900, or small, car-type vans. I have always thought there should be a market for a compact coachbuilt with a rising roof that would allow entry to multi-storey car parks as well as domestic garages — and beneath the 6ft 6in (2m) height barriers which are so beloved of local councils. I have suggested it to several manufacturers but have been treated with scorn. However, a recent hopeful sign has been the introduction of a trailer caravan with rising roof. The selling points are that it can be parked in an ordinary garage and offers less wind resistance on the move—attributes which would be welcomed by motorcaravanners.

How many people?

This is not really an important consideration, strange as it may seem, for the average family buying the average motorcaravan. The vast majority of motorcaravans have four or five berths and sitting places. Only large families and couples will have a limited choice. To accommodate one extra child, it is usually possible to have a stretcher bunk fitted across the cab. Lone caravanners can often save themselves a lot of cushion shuffling by leaving one bed permanently made up. Couples are badly served and must make do with motorcaravans built for four or five. A recent survey I made of the habits of some motorcaravan owners in the Caravan Club indicated that 80 per cent needed only two berths.

Towing a trailer?

Some claim that a motorcaravan plus trailer caravan gives the best of both worlds: more room and comfort on site, yet still the essential life-support systems when motoring solo. True, but mobility will be restricted and you will always have to return to base to pick up the trailer.

Nevertheless, a motorcaravan makes an excellent tug, for it is based on a rugged commercial chassis with an engine that is

The popular little Fiat 900 van has grown its first all-solid rising roof. The conversion is by Autohomes (UK) and is called 'Pandora'

(*above*) The car-like Mazda chassis with coachbuilt body by Riverside
(*below*) Suntrekker dismountable bodies for a Peugeot pickup truck

usually de-tuned and therefore not highly stressed. Maximum torque comes low down in the speed range, the clutch will withstand abuse and the final drive ratio is often geared lower than that of the equivalent car. All this adds up to the fact that steep hills and hill starts pose few problems and cruising speed and fuel consumption are little affected. That applies whether you are towing a trailer caravan, boat or load carrier.

There are, however, some motorcaravans that are better than others for towing. The front-engined, rear-wheel drive delivery van or chassis is favourite. The popular Volkswagen transporter, with a heavy rear engine which is air cooled, high-ratio third and top gears, ought in theory to be an awful tug, yet many old models

Here seen on a Fiat Strada, the Hitch Hiker dismountable will fit the majority of hatchback cars

can be seen coping with trailer caravans up to 16ft (4.9m) in length, albeit making slow progress up inclines, to the annoyance of following traffic. Naturally, the 2 litre VW is to be preferred to the 1600, and old 1600s kept in good order seem to get on better than the newer ones which, probably because of modern emission-control requirements, are thought by some owners to be a little sluggish.

Automatic transmission is no drawback—it can be a positive advantage in muddy fields—but, as with cars, it is advisable to fit an oil-temperature gauge, to keep an eye on it and to go in for an oil cooler if it proves necessary. Oil coolers sell well in the USA, where automatic transmission is the rule rather than the exception.

Coachbuilt motorcaravans make good tugs, in spite of their increased weight. I once towed a 10ft (3m) Sprite trailer caravan from the south of England to the north of Scotland with a Bedford Motorhome and had to keep reminding myself that it was still there. In the subsequent tour of the lanes of the Highlands it was an ideal set-up for two families. We travelled together but kept our own 'households' on site—rather more enjoyable than the time when we tried to cover the same ground in convoy, frequently losing sight of each other.

Towbars are freely available for the popular vans though modification to the rear step may be necessary. If a VW is to be so equipped, it is advisable to specify a towbar that goes to each side rather than beneath the engine. Most VW specialists seem to prefer to 'drop' the engine for anything other than minor work (though things are easier for mechanics on new VWs with their top access through a wide hatch). If the towbar has to be unbolted first, labour charges are inevitably increased.

Coachbuilts, with bodies that usually extend rearwards beyond the chassis, pose a bit of a problem. I know of no bolt-on towbars for them and it is usually a job for a specialist towbar manufacturer. Kits for the necessary electrical hook-ups are sold by motor and caravan accessory shops.

Single beds?

There are several reasons for motorcaravanners opting for single beds; some people simply prefer them and, of course, not all those who go camping are married couples. At least single beds eliminate the argument as to who should sleep against the wall.

Another of the quirks of motorcaravanning is that twin beds are most likely to be found in compact, front-engined delivery-van conversions, although some of the larger coachbuilts will have two doubles and a single. The reason is simple. Most British coachbuilts retain the original van cab and seats, over which the

An entirely conventional interior: Ford Trailblazer by Autohomes (UK). Settees may be converted to forward facing single seats

motorcaravan builders have installed a double bed in the Luton compartment. With a side door entrance, you will often find the kitchen, wardrobe and toilet compartment amidships, with a dinette/double bed across the rear. A variation is to put the dinette/double bed behind the cab, opposite the side entrance door. This has the advantage of providing forward- and rearward-facing seating in the middle of the caravan for travelling, which is more comfortable than inward-facing seats at the extreme rear. As this latter position is largely behind the rear wheels, the ride can be somewhat disturbing to those prone to travel sickness. It is also more sociable to have everybody within speaking distance when on the road. Coachbuilt motorcaravans with rear doors will have the seating towards the front, with work and washing areas at the rear.

There is not as much room in the way of length and width in conventional van conversions and manufacturers have been compelled to incorporate the cab seats into the sleeping arrangements, by reclining their backrests to the horizontal and making them the forward halves of single beds. Similar seats behind the cab have backrests flattened to mate with them, providing a pair of beds which are normally well over 6ft (1.8m) long, though on the offside the steering wheel with its column is the limiting factor. The gap between the single beds is sometimes bridged with cushions to make a giant double. If the interior of the van provides sufficient width, it is possible then to sleep across the vehicle and ignore the need to recline the front seats—or to flatten them anyway and treat them as 'roll-over' space.

The popular, rear engined VW van is converted by many manufacturers. Virtually all layouts are similar, with the rear bench seat changing into a bed which extends over the engine to the tailgate. I have seen only one with single beds, though many provide a double below and another beneath the rising roof.

Separate room for children?

Only the biggest coachbuilt motorhomes can provide two entirely separate bedrooms but, if the children are young, they can

Trailblazer seats in single-bed configuration. An enormous double can be made up by bridging the centre gangway.

The modern rear kitchen of a Holdsworth Renault Romance high top

be put to bed early in their own compartment with curtains drawn, and thus be effectivcly isolated. Many modern van conversions as well as coachbuilts now offer this opportunity. The once universal stretcher bunks along the sides are continued in a dwindling number of models. Though some rising roofs will accept only stretchers, virtually all modern Volkswagens benefit from an upper double bed because of a restriction imposed by the vehicle manufacturers in the way of a central roof bow which must not be removed if the guarantee is to remain intact. This has caused converters to scratch their heads and come up with some unusual solutions, most of which encompass an upholstered bed or beds of some sort where children can be isolated from what is going on down below.

If you have children whose bedtime comes before yours, it is a point worth bearing in mind when selecting a motorcaravan. Their sleeping space should be away from the door, so that parents can come and go without disturbing them. It must also be possible to use the kitchen and toilet room and gain access to the wardrobe without turfing them out of bed.

Complete motorcaravan?

A complete motorcaravan is one in which its occupants could live for a day or two, without stepping outside. It does not have to be big, though this would obviously make it more comfortable.

Most coachbuilt motorcaravans are now complete but there are still some secondhand models around that are not. A few high-top conversions of delivery vans offer everything necessary, including a walk-in toilet compartment (just), but you would not want to live completely within their four walls for long. It would be like life in the smallest DIY nuclear shelter.

Very many motorcaravans can, with a little ingenuity, be made virtually complete. Waste water tanks can be added beneath. Failing that, a collapsible tank may be easily connected to the sink outlet and carried in a kitchen cupboard. Keep it sweet with an occasional dose of disinfectant or bleach.

Today's small, flushing chemical closets are aesthetic to use and completely safe stored in a cupboard, or disguised as an extra seat. In an emergency, they can be put to their designed purpose within the vehicle whilst other occupants take a walk. Normally, of course, a separate toilet tent or lean-to annexe would provide privacy. There will be more about this in Chapters 7 and 11.

Cab armchairs on this Tabbert swivel to provide a lounge area which extends into the cab

Cruise van interior—sports obligatory wine goblets, TV set and plush upholstery. This is a Toyota Hi-Ace Cruisavan by Walkers

Other considerations

If many passengers are to be carried—children to school, the housebound on outings, or part of a football team—seats will be as important as beds. Cushions should be firmly located and, if journeys are to be long, most seats should face forwards. The Americans already insist, sensibly, that all seats occupied when travelling shall have safety belts. Europe lags behind. Asking if rear belts can be fitted will probably result in a rapid change of subject by the salesman. But it is possible, and a few enterprising coachbuilders and repairers are willing to undertake the task—at a price. Van conversions impose fewer problems than coachbuilts, which often employ a lot of wood in their construction, necessitating expensive reinforcement.

A motorcaravan provides a satisfying outlet for the activities of any DIY enthusiast and Chapter 6 is devoted to the subject. When selecting a vehicle, it is as well to bear in mind the loads it is going to have to carry in addition to passengers. It is difficult to get a standard 8 × 4ft (2,400 × 1,200mm) sheet of plywood through a side door. Rear access with a central corridor allows timber up to 12ft (3.6m) long to be carried in an ordinary van conversion. For most materials you are likely to want to collect from a DIY store, timber yard or builders' merchant, the 2ft (0.6m) wide rear door found on coachbuilts would be adequate but a furniture or antiques dealer would be better off with a panel van's twin rear doors. Businessmen and others who travel around collecting items of furniture will find a motorcaravan provides accommodation as well as load space but it might be better to have a 'special' built, or an existing model adapted, to suit the exact requirements.

Motorcaravans can be used in conjunction with most sports and leisure activities: fishing, rock climbing, pot-holing, gliding, ballooning, bird watching—the list is endless. They are ideal for dog shows and there are several 'travelling hotels' which provide accommodation for both horses and their riders. Some have dark-room facilities for photographers, others surgeries for travelling dentists; boats can be towed; balloonists and glider pilots who land away from base can be offered sustenance before their equipment is towed home. Whatever the need, there is a small but flourishing sideline in building motorcaravans for hundreds of different purposes.

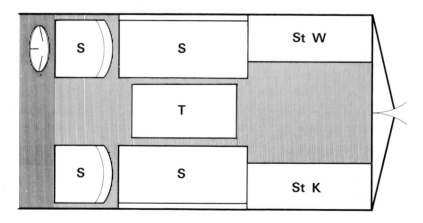

Conventional layout—converted van (see key, page 55)
Examples: Autohomes (UK), Auto-Sleepers, Holdsworth

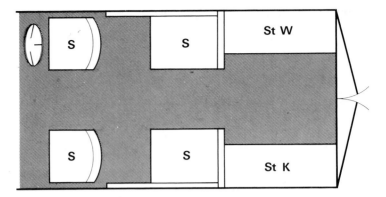

Converted van with face-forward rear seats

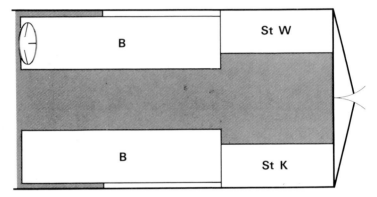

Converted van showing twin single beds. Front seats out of use

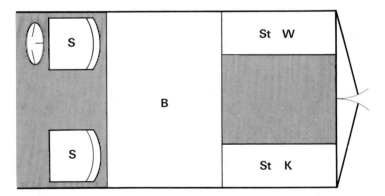

Converted van with transverse double bed. Front seats usable

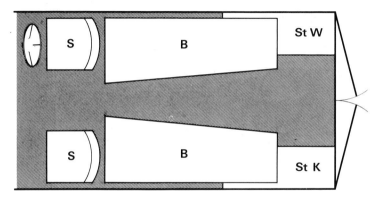

Converted van with upper stretcher bunks

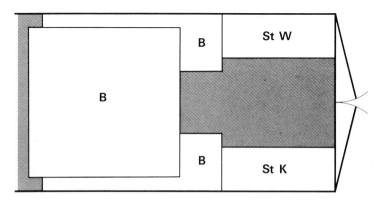

Converted van, rising roof or high top, with upholstered double bed. Example: Holdsworth

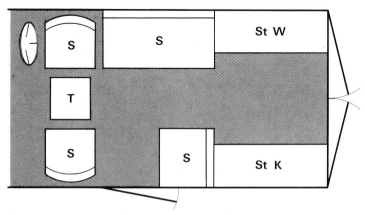

Converted van with side door and swivelling cab seats. Example: Holdsworth

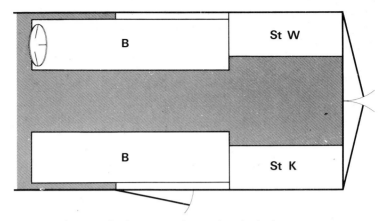

Converted van; side door out of use when beds down

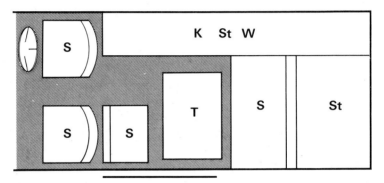

Examples: Autohomes (UK), Auto-Sleepers, Devon, Holdsworth, MI
Typical layout for side door Volkswagen Transporter.

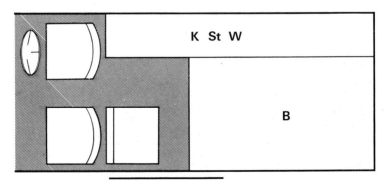

Volkswagen with bed in use. Side door and front seats remain usable

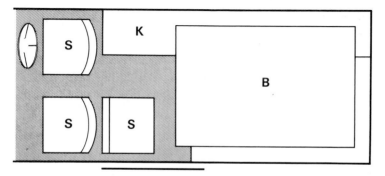

Volkswagen with upholstered roof bed at rear

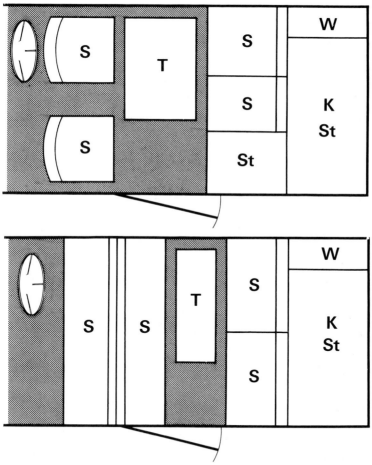

Typical layouts on Fiat and other small side-door vans. Rising roofs
provide extra beds by extending over one or both sides.
Examples: Autohomes (UK), M1

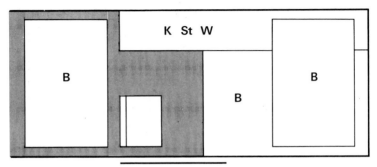

Roof beds in some Volkswagens may be split to provide two small transverse singles. Example: Devon

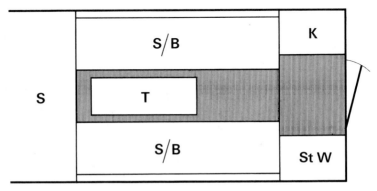

A small dismountable which gives standing space only in kitchen. Front storage space is above cab, hence seats always usable. Example: Romahome

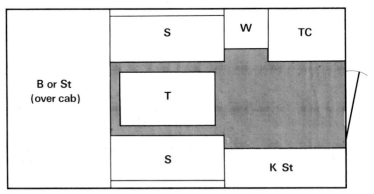

Coachbuilt with rear door and kitchen, day time. Example: Autohomes (UK)

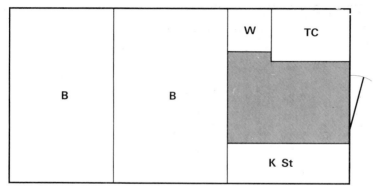

Coachbuilt with rear door and kitchen, night time. Cab seats usable, as with most coachbuilts.

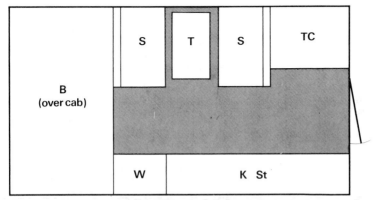

Coachbuilt with rear door and side kitchen, day.
Example: Autohomes (UK)

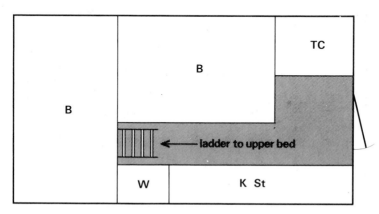

Coachbuilt with rear door and side kitchen, night.

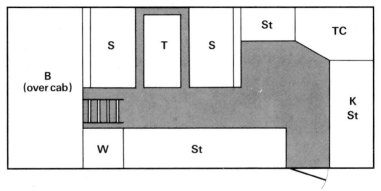

Coachbuilt with rear kitchen. Double bed. Example: Auto-Sleepers

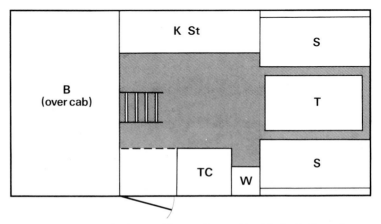

Coachbuilt with side door and rear dinette/double bed. Dotted line shows toilet extended across entrance. Examples: Advantura, Foster and Day, Glendale, G & T, Pioneer

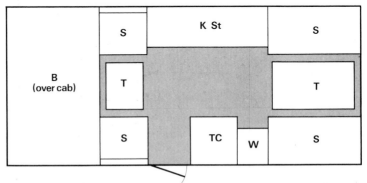

Large coachbuilt with transverse double and single dinettes/beds. Examples: Advantura, Foster and Day, Glendale, Pioneer

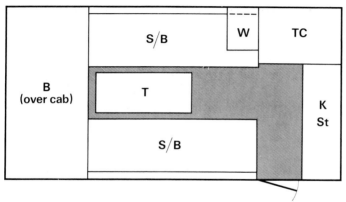

Compact coachbuilt with single beds. Wardrobe extends over offside bed. Example: Newlander

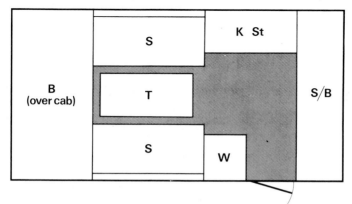

Compact coachbuilt with transverse double bed and single rear bed. Example: Newlander

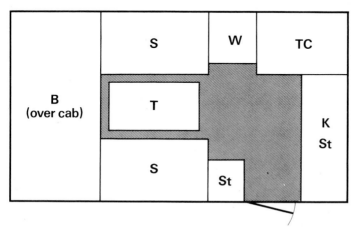

Compact coachbuilt on CDV chassis with transverse settee/double bed. Examples: Auto-Trail, Riverside, Glendale

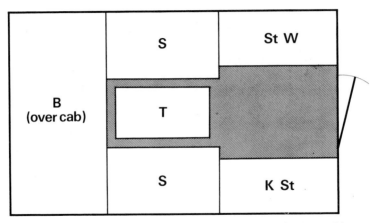

Dismountable body for CDV 1-ton pickup. Example: Suntrekker

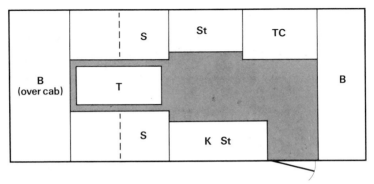

Coachbuilt with side door. Centre settees convert to face-forward seats. Example: Autohomes (UK)

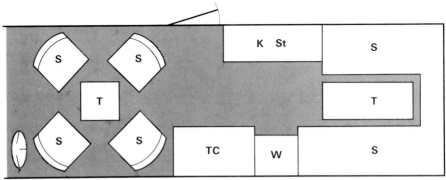

German A-class motorhome, daytime. Examples: Tabbert, Dethleff

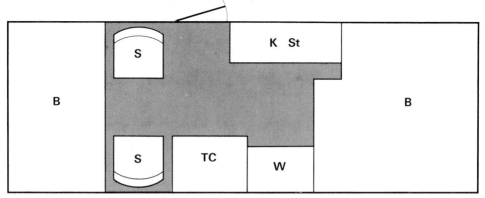

German A-class motorhome, night time. Front bed swings down from roof

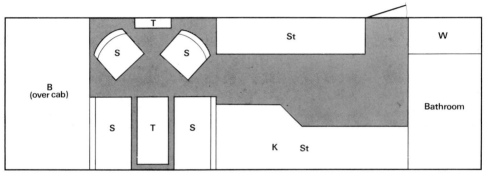

One of the many layouts available on American motorhomes.
Examples: Dudleys, Travel-Cruiser, Winnebago

Note Not all layouts illustrated in the drawings are in current production. Some may be found on secondhand motorcaravans. The following abbreviations are used:

B —bed or bunk   T —table
K —kitchen   TC—toilet compartment
S —seat   W —wardrobe
St—storage area

4
Which base vehicle?

It is safe to say that most vehicles in quantity production have, at some time or another, been made into motorcaravans. Among the more unusual bases, I have spotted a Rolls-Royce, Rover 3 litre, Austin signals van (from World War II and still running), Morris 1800 and Austin 1100. These all had purpose-made coachbuilt bodies. Conversions or adaptations have been made to a London taxi, VW Beetle, Morris Minor, scores of buses and coaches, one corporation dust cart, and hundreds of estate cars. This chapter will concentrate on the most popular base vehicles which are used by firms who have to sell their products to a critical public, ignoring the extremists.

Bedford

In alphabetical order, Bedford comes first with the CF range, introduced in October 1969, and still running, with minor modifications. The CF designation was dropped officially at the time of a major face-lift in 1980, when the bonnet was squared up and the small name plate at the front gave way to a big, bold 'BEDFORD' across the black radiator grille.

Most popular power unit is the 2.3 litre ohc engine from General Motors. It seems that motorcaravanners who have the smaller 1759cc option mostly wish they had chosen the other, having found that more power does not necessarily lead to a higher fuel consumption. The Bedford CF is notorious for the inaccessibility of the power unit, which is worked upon half under the bonnet and half from inside the cab. I have bitter memories of changing number 3 spark plug, lying on my side with excruciating cramp and fumbling by feel to get the thread started. As Bedford plugs should always be tightened with a torque wrench, this is a job I prefer to leave to the garage, or until the AA man turns up. In spite of the difficulties of servicing, the Bedford is without doubt the most popular van with DIY mechanics. These enthusiasts do everything that is in the book, and a lot that is not. This has been made somewhat less harrowing on the latest models, for the whole of the front panel is now completely removable.

Bedfords 'ripe for conversion': van, short and long wheelbase chassis-cabs

The 2.3 power unit is a beauty which will cruise all day and pull the motorcaravan smoothly up hills with an ability to hang on to top gear for longer than most of its rivals. The vehicle is one of the few with independent front suspension. Opinions are divided as to whether it is really worthwhile, for other makes manage to achieve an acceptable ride with cart springs and a beam axle. All Bedfords have an excellent lock but it is advisable to make full use of it only at slow speeds. Open the window and you will hear the tyres scrubbing the road—a very expensive noise. The steering was always good on directional stability at speed though rather heavy when parking, but later models seem to have overcome most of this difficulty.

The year 1969 saw the demise of the popular Bedford CA series, on which Dormobile made its famous name. The CA was an altogether different package: smaller, lower, more elegant and more car-like in driving position. It shared many components with the then current Vauxhall Victor car and, particularly in the early sixties, also one of its problems, namely rust. The CA had sliding doors to the cab. I saw one which, after being slammed shut by the driver, just went on travelling and ended up on the ground in front. The yearly vehicle test meant the graveyard for the worst CAs but Vauxhall–Bedford eventually overcame the rust problem and surviving examples are likely to be in good shape. They are now becoming collectors' treasures.

Other Bedford vans used occasionally by motorcaravan manufacturers include the little car-like HA with a 1256cc motor and
the KB25 or 26 imported since 1980 from Japan. The KB is a
pickup truck and makes a convenient carrier for the smaller
dismountable caravans. It has a 1584cc engine and, like most
Bedfords, the option of a diesel.

Daihatsu

Daihatsu's 55 wide van was first imported in 1979 and continues to
be available in limited numbers. It has a tiny 547cc, 2 cylinder
overhead camshaft motor beneath the floor which pushes it along
at a respectable road speed. It is a viable proposition for those
below average height. I found the cab very cramped and
involuntarily indicated a turn by knocking the stalk with my knee
every time I used the clutch. The 55 wide pickup will take a small
dismountable and return 40 miles to each gallon of petrol, or
more. There are longer, four-wheel drive Daihatsus with 1587cc
petrol or 2530cc diesel motors but they are used mainly by farmers
and have not exactly taken the motorcaravan manufacturers by
storm.

Datsun

Datsun E20/23 and the larger Cabstar vans and pickups are, like
the cars from the same factory, sensible, reliable pieces of
engineering without sparkle, although fully equipped with many
features which owners of European vehicles buy as extras. The big
snag is that they are in very short supply because of import
restrictions. The 4 cylinder ohv engine is mounted in the cab,
where three seats are provided. Make sure the centre seat is fitted
with a safety harness if you buy. Some of the earlier models,
imported in 1978, were not. There is also a car-like 1 ton pickup
with 1483cc (ohv) or 1770cc (ohc) engine which has been
imported since 1975 and has proved popular as a base for
dismountable bodies and (attached) coachbuilts.

Dodge

The Dodge began life as the Commer in 1960 and continued
virtually unchanged during its twenty-one year life span, apart
from a bit of front grille badge engineering and improvements to
interior trim. When it became a Dodge it was referred to,

58

Last version of the popular Commer/Dodge before its demise in 1981

justifiably, as the 'Spacevan'. Offering more internal width and length than any of its contemporaries, it was naturally popular with motorcaravan converters, although the engine, located between the front wheels and in line with the cab seats, imposed certain limitations upon interior design.

The Commer was much sought after when it first became available to motorcaravan manufacturers in the early sixties, being altogether more sophisticated and having lighter controls than its rivals—chief among them being the Austin-Morris (see Leyland). Using many components from the old Humber Hawk car, it was well tried even when first introduced; it suffered few teething troubles and remained a reliable if rather uninteresting package until its demise in 1981. In its latter days, the Commer sold mainly on its low price, being able to offer a lot of motorcaravan for comparatively little money.

The pickup version was seldom available on the retail market. Motorcaravan manufacturers ordered special chassis–cab versions on which to build coachbuilts. The Commer Highwayman was seen everywhere at one time and continued into the seventies.

No outstanding defects have come to light. It is advisable to keep petrol and air filters clean and, if the flame trap is disconnected it is essential to remount it the right way round. Some unadaptable drivers did not like the handbrake, mounted to the offside of the driver's seat. When jacking remember that, although the vehicle has rear-wheel drive, the handbrake operates on the front wheels.

Scores of happy owners were sad to see the series dropped but there are many secondhand models around and spares and servicing will be available for a long time. A drive-away front end was listed from 1960. It is a pity some enterprising manufacturer did not seize the chance to offer the British public the first economical class A motorhome. With no cab to cut away, the whole body could have been designed as a motorhome from the wheels up.

The Commer is the subject of more name confusion than even the products of British Leyland. It was produced by Rootes, who were taken over by Chrysler, who eventually put the Dodge badge on. Now, owners will look for servicing and spares under the Talbot designation, except in Europe where Simca dealers could still prove helpful, although in remote areas you might still spot the historical names of Sunbeam, Humber, Hillman or Karrier.

Fiat

The Fiat 850T, 900T and 900E models are all basically the same, with a 903cc ohv engine mounted at the rear like the Volkwagen's, except that the Fiat's is water cooled and entirely conventional. Measuring just a little more than 12ft (3.6m) in length, it is a delightful little package that can be treated like a small car. Comfort and interior trim have been improved immeasurably over the years since it was first imported in 1970. So has rust proofing, which was rather poor at first. Very few privately converted models were ever produced because it was always a difficult van to track down at Fiat car-dealer showrooms. Some have been telling potential customers for years that the model had been discontinued, but it is still around and still being imported by two large motorcaravan manufacturers.

Apart from rust, some early motorcaravans were subject to a bit of body distortion. Check that all doors close fairly and squarely before buying. Go for a run, too, with a passenger in the rear. Ingress of exhaust fumes has been another frequent cause of complaint but is fairly easy to cure provided the doors are fitting tightly. The 900T models were often subject to a squeal from the brakes. It is not important; you can learn to live with it. A temporary cure can be effected by de-dusting drums and chamfering edges of linings. It is not advisable to attempt brake adjustment unless you are adept with a feeler gauge. This is a fiddly process, best left to the experts. DIY maintenance of an ambitious nature is not encouraged by Fiat UK and works manuals are difficult to obtain. But do not be put off. If the caravan is big enough for you, you will enjoy the motoring and the Fiat will tackle anything. Alpine passes and the steeper hills in Scotland and Wales can be stormed with ease.

There is a much bigger Fiat called the Daily. It has a very smooth 2.5 litre diesel engine and drives like a petrol model. It is used in very small numbers for motorcaravan conversion— mainly 'one-offs'. The Fiat Iveco is similar to the Talbot Express.

Ford

The Ford Transit created quite a sensation when first launched in 1965 as a replacement for the much smaller Thames with 1700cc Consul engine. Many motorcaravanners thought it big and ugly but it soon became a favourite and remains so today.

Transits have often been at a slight disadvantage because of a price differential but, for the extra money, the owner got a cab that was a cut above those of its contemporaries, with less of the delivery van feel about it. The original Transits had Ford V-4 engines of 1600 or 2000cc capacity which made the space under the snub bonnet somewhat cramped. There was also a rather sluggish in-line 'Kent' engine of 1598cc available during the mid-seventies. It was alleged to be more economical than the somewhat thirsty V-4 but motorcaravan owners found that they did not achieve any significant improvement in fuel consumption because the engine had to work harder to give the performance expected. By the end of 1978 the V-4 engines had been phased out, to be replaced with in-line ohc motors of about the same capacities. There was now much more room beneath the new, squared-up bonnet and, more important, an improvement in miles per gallon.

Older Transits occasionally blew cylinder-head gaskets but

there have been no significant trends in the way of recurring faults in any of the models. Controls are fairly light. Some owners complain of heavy steering at slow speeds but I suspect this is often lack of attention to maintenance and tyre pressures. On the whole, Transits have rather light steering when motoring—too light, in the opinion of many. The 'Transit wander' is as well acknowledged a phenomenon as the 'Bedford bounce' caused by tired shock absorbers. Transit steering does need careful adjustment from time to time by the experts. Strangely enough, among the many Transits I have driven, the tendency to wander has been more pronounced on those with van bodies than the bigger coachbuilts. This could be because the latter are normally built on chassis with stronger springs and tougher shocks, designed to cope with the extra loading.

Transit-mounted coachbuilts can cost up to £1,000 more than Bedford equivalents. For that you get a superior cab with comfortable seats (three-way adjustment on the driver's), a more accessible engine and superior noise insulation. Bedfords are now doing their best, belatedly, to catch up and you will still find a bigger choice of Bedfords than Fords.

If you see an old-shape Transit with a bull nose, it is either a diesel or a rather rare beast, a V-6 with 3 litre engine taken from Ford's top of the range car, the Granada. They were produced in limited numbers over the years and gave sparkling performance at the expense of fuel economy. It is a costly luxury to be able to see cars growing smaller in the rear-view mirror of a big coachbuilt.

Fords have also produced the little, car-like Escort van since 1968, with engines between 1 and 1.6 litres. A few were made into mini-motorcaravans by established converters but the new, 1980, range does not seem to be suitable. Like the small cars with the same badge, it is a good little vehicle for economical motoring, with no serious or repetitive faults. The Cortina-based P100 pickup is used as a base for dismountables.

Honda

Honda is another Japanese midget, in van and pickup form. The one with four headlamps, the TN7, is smaller than its successor, the Acty. The earlier model, imported from 1976, gave reasonable performance from its 354cc, ohc, 2 cylinder water-cooled, underfloor engine. It was used chiefly as a base for dismountable

Compact Romahome dismountable body on a Honda pickup truck. Rear overhang provides standing room in the kitchen

bodies, although one enterprising if over-ambitious manufacturer did mount a 6ft (1.8m) wide coachbuilt body on the poor little thing. Not surprisingly, few were produced.

Although my wife and I found the cab of the TN7 almost unbearably small (having to dismount to stretch legs every hour) we enormously enjoyed a few days' testing of the newer Acty with a 545cc motor. It is a thoroughly practicable proposition for those with limited means. We know a couple, now on the retirement register and accustomed to coping with larger and nobler machinery, who are delighted with their little buzz–bomb. It took them, loaded with full caravan equipment, plus a tent, up a 1 in 3 hill unexpectedly encountered in Devon; and it consistently returns 45mpg unless pushed really hard. The Acty has all the sophistication of modern motorcars, including an electric radiator fan which comes on only when it is needed. Like other Japanese products, it has a reputation for reliability — which is just as well, as you have to go through the floor of the caravan to reach the engine, although oiling and watering points are located accessibly.

Leyland

The four-wheel drive Land Rover is a vehicle apart. For motorcaravanners it is available in limited numbers, usually in the form of the station wagon made into a caravan, though the pickup can occasionally be seen carrying a dismountable body. The specialists who buy it will know exactly what they are looking for so we will pass straight to Leyland's most popular vehicle for motorcaravan conversion.

The Sherpa, now marketed under the Freight Rover banner, was entirely re-vamped in 1982 and now comes with a 1700 or 2000 ohc motor. First introduced in 1974 with a 1622cc ohv engine, the most popular version with motorcaravanners has had the much loved 1800cc motor—the ultimate development of the Austin-Morris 'B' series engine, for long used in Cambridge and Oxford cars and MG 'B' GT Sportsters. The 'B' engine gained a well deserved reputation for reliability coupled with better-than-the-others fuel economy. There were teething troubles when the 1700cc ohv 'O' series engine was introduced in the late seventies but, as far as motorcaravanners are concerned, the optional 2000cc engine now fitted is a different proposition which gives sparkling performance coupled with excellent economy and, apparently,

Suntrekker 204 dismountable on Land Rover—a go-anywhere-in-comfort vehicle

reliability. I would say you could snap up any older model with the 1800 engine with no hesitation but would advise looking for signs of oil leaks on a 1700.

Early Sherpas had heavy steering which gave excellent directional stability at speed but made for arm-wrenching work when trying to shuffle into a tight parking space. Steering has grown progressively lighter over the years, without apparent loss of directional stability. In my experience, the Sherpa has always sat on the road more firmly than its rivals, even when encumbered with a big, overhanging coachbuilt body. Brakes have always been up to scratch although older models have been known to judder alarmingly when anchors were thrown out at speed. The first time it happened to me I thought I was down to the shoes and drove very carefully until they were checked. De-dusting and a roughening of the linings cured the trouble for the next 10,000 miles.

Even the beloved 1800 engine can be subject to a bit of oil creepage, according to my experience and that of other owners. Though oil consumption is virtually nil, minute quantities can creep through to the clutch, producing an effect similar to the juddering brakes. The only cure is expensive in labour—a new clutch plate. But you should get 20–25,000 miles between renewals. When buying a secondhand Sherpa, check the clutch for smooth operation. A temporary cure can sometimes, by the way, be effected by violent and deliberate slipping of the clutch.

Nearly all Sherpas suffered from rust at the horizontal seams on the bodywork, the lower seams naturally being affected most. It is cosmetic and non-structural but can look awful. The rust can be covered with stick-on rubbing strakes but, unless properly treated, will go on creeping undetected. The 1982 models were completely redesigned, with vertical seams which should abolish the problem.

The new Sherpa with 2000cc engine is one of the liveliest yet quietest little motorcaravans I have driven. After lagging behind the competition in the way of ergonomics and creature comforts for years, Leyland has now, following a reorganisation, apparently leapt ahead. There are more options offered than by many others, such as four-wheel drive, limited slip differential, overdrive, and gas conversion, as well as the diesel alternative available to order on most popular light vans.

Before the Sherpa there were other Leyland Austin-Morris vans used for conversion. The Austin 152 had a straight front grille, the Morris J2's had curves in the outline. Apart from that the two were identical, with between-seats engine and a sloppy steering-column gear change which eventually was replaced by a floor mounted, remote control stick. They both used the famous 'B' series engine in 1489cc form. A direct descendant was the 250JU which had the engine increased to 1622cc and mounted beneath the cab floor, tilted half-way on to its side. The 250JU, 152 and J2 all had the same body, nearly 9ft (2.7m) long and 6ft (1.8m) wide at the floor, though the waist was considerably less. The 250JU ran from 1967 to 1974 when it was discontinued, with no direct replacement.

Running concurrently with these three was the J4, a more compact vehicle with the same mechanical layout. It was replaced by the Sherpa which looked, in fact, like a J4 with a bonnet stuck on the front. The J4, being compact, had possibilities which were never developed. If only the engineers had sorted out the heavy steering which it shared with its larger brothers, the ergonomists the appalling seating and the stylists the dreary paintwork, it could still have been in the running. But I will never understand why Leyland failed to develop the so successful front-wheel drive 1800 cars for the commercial field. It had, without knowing it, the makings of a van which could have pre-dated the acclaimed Renault Trafic by at least ten years.

Leyland has always been in the running with its small car-derived vans and the first basis for a compact motorcaravan conversion was the Austin $\frac{1}{2}$ ton van, derived directly from the Cambridge. With the arrival of the Marina came the better looking Marina van, which reverted to a number when Marina became Ital. They are unexciting but reliable and economical little vans, with no particular faults though there was, at one time, a reputation for an unduly large number of Friday (hurriedly assembled) cars being produced.

MAN-VW

MAN-VW is the designation given to the larger VW LT vans, because they are handled by truck specialists, not car dealers. Unlike the familiar Volkswagens, these big boys have 1984cc water-cooled engines (from the Audi car range) mounted at the

Suntor conversion on Leyland's CDV Marina van. Latest versions have side-lift rising roof

MAN-VW LT (left) and VW Transporter, converted and photographed in the Cotswolds by Auto-Sleepers

front and driving the rear wheels. They were introduced to Britain in 1975 and have earned a reputation for reliability. Chassis cabs (for coachbuilts) and diesel engines (2710cc) are popular with motorcaravan manufacturers. A more powerful petrol engine and other refinements were added in 1983.

Mazda

Mazda have imported car-like pickups from 1973, first with a 1600cc engine, expanded to 1800cc in 1977. These trucks are used to carry dismountables.

Mercedes-Benz

Mercedes-Benz introduced the L206D front-wheel drive diesel van in 1973 and it was immediately and justifiably popular with converters at the top end of the price range. Its only real snag seems to be an overlarge turning circle, corrected when the replacement 207D arrived in 1977 with rear-wheel drive. These vehicles have a well-deserved reputation for rugged reliability and it is difficult to find a secondhand version because owners tend to hold on to them. You have only to step into the cab of a Merc, closing the door with a satisfying 'clunk', to feel the impression of quality and solidity.

I thought the 207D was the best, until I had a 208 (now 210) on test for a week. This is the petrol version, first imported in 1980,

Renault Trafic front-wheel-drive vans with Holdsworth conversions. Left to right: short wheelbase high top; short wheelbase rising roof; long wheelbase high top

with a 2307cc engine producing 85 bhp as opposed to the 2404cc diesel and its 65 bhp. It is quieter, livelier and altogether more pleasant to drive than anything I have tried from Europe or Japan.

The Mercedes 300 and 400 series vans and chassis are longer versions of the same base vehicles, with the same engines—which can begin to feel a trifle underpowered if a big coachbuilt body is fitted.

Mitsubishi
Mitsubishi provides a nice compact little van or pickup in the Colt, imported since 1979, with a conventional 1597cc ohc engine beneath the third front seat. It is in very short supply and one enterprising coachbuilder had to abandon the motorcaravans he was building because of non-availability of chassis.

Renault
The Renault Trafic came from France in 1981 and was hailed as the answer to a motorcaravanner's prayer, having more desirable features within compact overall dimensions than most others. The main attraction of the extensive range is the number of variations available on a theme: front- or rear-wheel drive, diesel or petrol, standard or high top, long or short wheelbase. The front-drive high top is particularly suitable for motorcaravan conversion, providing a low floor that needs no step, 6ft (1.8m) of headroom and full-height rear doors that demand no stooping. All models have a side door, which increases versatility. Engine options are 1397cc and 1647cc petrol and 2068cc diesel. The Master is a larger version of the Trafic, with 1995cc petrol engine or 2445cc diesel. I enjoyed driving the Trafic with the smaller engine, found it particularly light on the controls, easy to manoeuvre and livelier than you would expect from less than 1400cc. There were no discernible shortcomings.

Suzuki
Suzuki ST80 and ST90 midgets were first imported in 1979. Vans are converted to tiny motorcaravans and pickups carry dismountable bodies. Suzuki is the small one with the largest engine, all of 797cc, located beneath the floor. Performance is sparkling; it is a real fun vehicle, though in short supply.

The promising new Talbot Express high top with Auto-Sleeper conversion

Talbot

The Talbot Express was introduced to the British market late in 1982 and first, rushed caravan conversions appeared at the November Caravan Show. This likely-looking front-wheel drive vehicle from Italy has not been around long enough in motorcaravan form for any significant reports to have reached me. It is available as a standard van, a high-roof van or chassis-cab in both long and short wheelbase versions. The smallest model, the 1000, has a petrol engine of 1796cc and four-speed gearbox. Larger 1300 and 1500 models have 1971cc petrol engines and five-speed gearboxes. A 2500cc diesel engine is one of the options.

Toyota

The Toyota Hi-Ace van was imported from 1973, at first specifically for motorcaravan conversion. Early models had four headlamps and hard cab seats. The later, re-styled model was better looking and arrived late 1977. Pickup and chassis-cab versions are available, so Toyotas can be found carrying dismountables, with coachbuilt bodies or as converted vans with rising roofs or high tops. Owners seem happy with their Toyotas, remarking on the general absence of problems between services

Toyota Hi-Ace van—a good-looker in short supply

but a few have complained of starting difficulties with a warm engine. There are three engine options: 1587cc ohv and 1968cc ohc petrol and 2188cc diesel. There is also the four-wheel drive Land Cruiser pickup with 6 cylinder 4 litre engine—a direct rival to the Land Rover. The smaller Hi-Lux car-like pickup with 1587cc engine will also take a small dismountable body. 1983 saw the introduction of a sleek new van with 1812cc petrol engine.

Volkswagen

Volkswagen started it all soon after the war, with its adaptation of the rear-engined and economical 'people's car'—a simple concept which proved to be just what the people wanted. The rather noisy air-cooled engine was hidden away at the rear. With muffled insulation and cushions on seats, it provided, and still provides, a quieter run than most front-engined vans. Volkswagen's policy of setting up service centres and stocks of spares before launching the product on any particular market contributed to its reputation, which was based upon reliability stemming from thorough inspection of each vehicle before it left the German factory. In the days when 'running in, please pass' was a common slogan seen on rear windows, all VW engines were run in at the factory.

71

The first Volkswagens had a 1200cc flat-four engine. It has gradually been expanded to 1584cc with a 1973cc petrol or 1586cc diesel option. The VW reputation lives on in spite of a tendency (reported by several owners) for number 3 cylinder on some 1600 engines to run hot and cause valve failure (can be expensive).

There have been two major changes to bodies. In the mid-sixties, the original two-piece windscreen and twin-hinged side doors were phased out in favour of a curved windscreen and sliding door. In 1979 a smart new body shape was introduced and the spare wheel was placed beneath the front floor. Official location for previous spares had been inside the vehicle, hence the proliferation of devices for getting it out of the way above the front bumper or, more unusually, slung at the rear.

The 1600cc engines in these new models have redesigned valves and there should be no overheating problems. But many motorcaravans are now fitted with the 2000cc engine, which gives superior performance yet makes very little difference to the touring fuel consumption. The 1600 is thought by many to be too sluggish for today's needs; others defend it vehemently. One thing is certain: spares for the larger engine seem disproportionately more expensive but perhaps, as its popularity increases, their relative cost may be reduced, or not increased so rapidly. Now air-cooled VWs are being phased out, to be replaced with an even quieter 1900cc, water-cooled, flat-four engine at the rear.

Volkswagens for motorcaravans begin life as vans, Kombis or microbuses. The latter have superior trim and finish, which often shows in the completed motorcaravan. Considering the number in use, there seem to be very few complaints about VWs. The commonest grumble is about cab heating on the older 1600cc models. By the time the engine's waste heat has been blown by a fan right to the front through ducting, there is not much of it left. All VWs have tight fitting doors. It is this effective body sealing which makes it so difficult to raise an elevating roof if doors and windows are all closed. On the same basis, the blown hot air should stand a better chance of getting into the passenger compartment if a window is opened slightly. If that does not work, it means an expensive new exhaust system, for that is where the hot air comes from. Consistent with Volkswagen's policy of gradual improvement rather than frequent radical changes, heating on the new models seems to give no problems.

Average petrol consumptions

How on earth does one choose a base vehicle from such a bewildering array? The final choice will depend on a mixture of personal prejudice, servicing and spares availability and whatever the ideal caravan happens to be mounted upon. If you are starting from scratch, ordering just what you want, the accompanying table of petrol consumptions may influence you. It has been compiled from figures supplied by practising motorcaravanners (readers of *Motorcaravan & Motorhome Monthly*) over a year or so and is based upon mileages as recorded by the vehicles' odometers. Remember that heavy coachbuilt bodies will usually increase consumption by 10–20 per cent, according to the way you drive.

	mpg	*litres/100 Km*
Bedford 1600 conversions (includes later CA models)	23.74	11.89
Bedford 2300 conversions	23.97	11.78
Bedford 2300 coachbuilts	20.42	13.83
Commer/Dodge 1724cc conversions	22.53	12.53
Fiat 850/900T conversions	33.08	8.53
Ford Transit V4 2 litre conversions	20.98	13.46
Ford Transit V4 2 litre coachbuilts	20.47	13.80
Ford Transit ohc 2 litre conversions	22.25	12.69
Ford Transit ohc 2 litre coachbuilts	22.27	12.68
Ford Transit V6 coachbuilts	16.20	17.44
Freight Rover Sherpa 1800 conversions	25.02	11.29
Freight Rover Sherpa 1700 conversions	27.60	10.23
Freight Rover Sherpa 1700 conversions with overdrive	26.20	10.78
Land Rover 2.6 litre conversions	20.95	13.48
Mercedes 207D conversions (diesel)	29.16	9.69
Toyota 1600 conversions	29.18	9.68
Toyota 2000 conversions	27.21	10.38
VW 1600 conversions	25.37	11.13
VW 2000 conversions	23.62	11.96
VW LT 2 litre conversions	18.37	15.38

US models

The American vehicles imported in limited numbers are Chevy, Dodge and Ford. I have driven several and could hardly tell the difference between them, for they all provide absolutely effortless motoring. All the driver has to do is steer, and that is usually power assisted. Petrol consumption can be as high as 7mpg or around 18–20mpg, according to body size and driving habits. The big, lazy engines should last well but it is advisable to ask searching questions about spares and servicing.

As with cars these days, there are no 'bad' vehicles (except perhaps for a few obscure models which creep beneath the Iron Curtain occasionally). Every factory, despite automation, manages to produce the odd rogue or Friday model. There will be more about how and what to buy in the next chapter but bear in mind the availability of servicing and spares. This applies equally to the big V8s from America and the tiny Japanese models. It can be aggravating to have to travel far for routine servicing, or spares if you are able to do the work yourself. Many franchised garages may refuse to work on unconventional vehicles and even the friendly AA or RAC men could be baffled, resourceful though most of them are.

5
Buying and selling

After digesting Chapters 3 and 4 you will, it is hoped, have some idea of which types of motorcaravans you could live in and which base vehicles can be placed on your short list. If you are a complete newcomer to the game, I would suggest that it is virtually essential to spend several hours, days even, visiting showrooms and just sitting in many motorcaravans, preferably in the company of the rest of the family. It could also be helpful to visit, with prior permission, a motorcaravan rally of one of the clubs. Members will be happy to chat with you.

First comes a quick walk round the whole sales area, merely looking through windows and getting a rough idea of what is available. This is followed by a more detailed assimilation of models that interest you. Just sit there for five minutes or so to see whether the general ambience is to your liking, or could be made so with a few minor changes, a new set of curtains, for instance.

Then try the cab seats and travelling positions for the rest of the family, asking for comments. If passengers are to travel in the rear, they will need seats that remain firmly located and have safety harnesses. There is a thousand-to-one chance against finding the latter and, if this worries you, it is as well to consider possible mounting points at this stage. Most run-of-the-mill van conversions do not pose too much of a problem and clubs or magazines should be able to supply addresses of one or two firms able to undertake the work. But they are few and far apart. Coachbuilts with wooden floors and bodies pose more of a problem because extensive reinforcement is often necessary. When choosing a motorcaravan, just remember that lap belts require two anchorage points at floor level, for seats or seat boxes themselves are seldom strong enough to take the strain. As correspondence over the years has shown, responsible parents are concerned about the absence of anchorage points for harnesses or child safety seats. Legislation has lagged far behind demand and even if compulsion comes on new models, it will be a decade or two before rear seat belts become the norm.

In the initial stages of choosing a motorcaravan, it is advisable to visit the premises of several traders and, whilst examining their stocks, assess the dealers themselves. Ask a few pertinent questions about after-sales work and guarantees. Compared with the number of garages selling cars, motorcaravan dealers are thin on the ground and visiting just a few showgrounds will involve a spot of travelling. As most of them are open at weekends (some with restricted hours and sales facilities on Sundays) this should pose no undue problems, although it is much easier if you have your own transport. The latter may be the vehicle you hope to trade in part exchange and, at this stage, it is worth asking about allowances — just another of the many factors to be taken into consideration before making the final choice of dealer, let alone motorcaravan. It will soon become apparent that the lowest priced new or secondhand motorcaravan may not represent the best bargain.

The balance you have to find, representing the difference between the price of the new motorcaravan and the allowance on yours, is a major but by no means the only consideration. In my many transactions, I have found it pays to shop locally and am now prepared to pay a little over the odds if necessary for the convenience of doing so. Locally, in this respect, means within convenient travelling distance over a route well served by public transport, or it may be nearer to the place of work than home. It is also worth noting that practically any motorcaravan will carry a push bike or moped. This can give a measure of independence if the repair or service turns out to be a long job.

Experience has taught me that something invariably needs attention after buying a vehicle, whether new or secondhand, and you should ascertain what is to be done about it before agreeing to anything. Very few motorcaravan dealers have workshop facilities for dealing with any but the most minor faults on the vehicle but the seller is responsible in law for these as much as for the caravan part. Find out what the procedure is. Usually you will be authorised to go to your nearest franchised garage.

Some motorcaravan sales outlets have extensive workshops for the repair of anything to do with the caravan and, in addition to the essential pre-delivery check, can carry out ambitious modifications and install any other equipment needed. Others have merely an odd-job man with a tool kit who expects to spend most of his time washing vehicles and cleaning them inside and out prior to sale. The best of these dealers liaise closely with local specialists who can install extra equipment or make good defects. But there is usually nobody on the premises capable of putting something right on the spot. Again, it is essential to establish the procedure should anything go wrong.

When you have selected your dealer and are down to what appears to be the ideal motorcaravan for your purposes (or, more likely, the best compromise that can be found at the right price), then is the time to spend an uninterrupted hour with it, going over everything with a fine tooth comb. But I prefer the demonstration run at this stage. If you can take a knowledgeable mechanically minded friend with you, so much the better. If not, ask about AA or RAC inspection. You may decide that it is not necessary but the seller's attitude to such a request can be revealing. Do not be fobbed off with stories about your common-law rights, which are drawn up to ensure that customers receive 'goods of merchantable quality' that are fit for the purpose for which they were bought. Putting these into effect can involve an awful lot of aggravation if the seller decides not to cooperate and you will be happier dealing with a firm who will undertake the responsibility of righting any wrongs, without argument or recourse to law.

On the demonstration run, which should be long enough to warm the engine thoroughly, the salesman will probably take off from his premises, then hand over to you. If he does not, ask. Accept no excuses about insurance. Provided you have a current driving licence, his insurance will cover you, and if he is too mean to have full business insurance, you would stand little chance of getting anything out of him in the way of after-sales backup.

During your drive, try everything. Do not forget to slam on the brakes (after looking in the mirror and giving passengers due warning). Try changing down through the gears as well as up and, if possible, attack a hill to see how the vehicle pulls. Stop at the steepest part and restart, to check handbrake and clutch for smooth operation. The severest test of the clutch and transmission comes when reversing up a steep slope. This may not be possible but a partial simulation can be effected by reversing a short distance with the handbrake lightly applied. If the caravan has a re-frigerator which works on 12V as well as gas, switch it on before the test run. It will not freeze or make ice in this short distance but the freezer unit should at least feel a little colder to the touch than the inside of the rest of the cabinet.

After the test run dismiss the salesman and spend a considerable amount of time going over (and under) the whole motorcaravan, making a list of any defects spotted. Examine the outside first. Lie on your back and slide underneath (fortunately most light commercial vans have good ground clearance) and be thankful that you have either brought an overall or are not wearing your best clothes. Look for traces of seepage from petrol, water and waste-water tanks and examine all pipework (petrol, brake and water) for signs of wear or chafing. Note any signs of rust, particularly on the hidden sides of sills. Any attempt to botch with glass fibre or tape and a bit of paint will be more apparent from the side you are not meant to look at. I always treat sills that have been painted black or in contrast to the rest of the bodywork with suspicion. It could have been done by a previous owner because he thought it improved the appearance but matt-black paint will hide a multitude of sins because it does not reflect the light.

A bit of rust on sills is unlikely to be structural but rust elsewhere, especially on floor, chassis or exhaust system, could be serious and calls for an expert, independent opinion such as A A or RAC inspection. Whilst underneath, check the spare wheel. On some vehicles it is so inaccessible as to be forgotten during normal dealer services. I must admit that I ignored my own advice on my last purchase. I knew the dealer to have a reputation for honesty and reliability and assumed this little matter would be attended to during the pre-delivery check. Subsequently, I found the spare to be completely unused and absolutely devoid of air. As it now shows no signs of losing the 40 psi that I put in, it would seem that it had never been checked during the vehicle's three years of life, although a record of routine services by accredited dealers came with the vehicle.

Still underneath, look for signs of seepage from shock absorbers and examine the walls of the tyres for cracks or bulges. Ensure that any underfloor tanks are not sited dangerously near the exhaust pipe or brake lines. Then wriggle out and inspect the outside walls and treads of the tyres before standing up and turning your attention to the exterior bodywork.

At this stage, if there is a rising roof, put it up. Look for signs of gaps at seams and joints of the sidewalls. Flexible walls, being made of plastic, are easy to wash if the job has been done regularly but, if dirt and stains are allowed to remain they can be impossible to shift and replacement of the material is the only solution.

Try all doors and opening windows. They should operate without undue effort and close completely and easily. Ill-fitting doors and absence of a small part of their seals can cause exhaust fumes to enter the interior. This is the cause of many complaints about conversions of the little Fiat van. If the motorcaravan is a coachbuilt, ensure that the exhaust pipe has been extended so that it clears the body.

Then stand away from the vehicle, which should be on level ground. From front and back notice whether it stands level or leans to one side, caused perhaps by positioning all the heavy items on one side. Look along each side and make a note of any bulges or wrinkles in the outer skin. Next, stand back and assess whether there is any pronounced droop to front or rear. Coachbuilts with overcab compartments are sometimes nose heavy. This can be caused by carrying too many heavy items like folding chairs and television sets up there. I have known people (who do not use the bed) put a couple of spare wheels in the overcab—convenient, certainly, but not the place for heavy loads which can affect springs and handling.

Van conversions are more likely to have been used as dual-purpose work horses. That is all right if the previous owner was, say, a florist, but a builder or market gardener would have been tempted at times to carry heavier things than bunches of flowers, so look for signs of rear-end droop. Some motorcaravans are converted on secondhand vehicles which have already served the first part of their lives as tradesmen's vans. The registration document may or may not give a clue but in any case examine particularly thoroughly anything which has an obviously new conversion on an older base vehicle.

Deliberate deception on the part of motorcaravan dealers is rare. The penalties for 'clocking' the mileage indicator are severe. It is not so much the fine as the resultant publicity that is the effective deterrent. Usually salesmen are willing to discuss previous history and ownership and I have had telephone calls from potential buyers of motorcaravans which I have part exchanged. One related to a vehicle I had sold five years previously.

When you are looking at the sides, take note of the positions of the fuel filler and refrigerator vents. They should be nowhere near each other. If they are, *never* motor with gas alight. It is a dangerous practice anyway.

Have a nose around beneath the bonnet or in the engine compartment. If oil, water and battery levels are low, suspect neglect. Oil on the dipstick and water in the header tank should be free from signs of contamination, and battery terminals should be free from corrosion. Check plug leads for signs of cracks and feel the water hoses, which should be firm and not spongy. The fan belt must be sound and at the correct tension—about $\frac{1}{2}$in (1cm) of movement when pressed fairly hard midway between two pulleys.

Get a volunteer to sit in the driver's seat so that you can remain outside and check correct working of all lights and indicators, while the one in the cab notices whether the appropriate warning lights are working. Start the engine and see how long the low oil-pressure indicator lamp takes to go out—more than two or three seconds could indicate the need for pump replacement. In addition to lights and gauges in the cab, do not forget to test windscreen wipers and washers, instrument lights and the door-operated courtesy lamp if one is fitted.

Sit inside the caravan for a few minutes to get the feel of the thing, then open and close all doors and drawers, making sure that their catches hold securely and that hinges are not strained. Next, make up the beds, ensuring that all the pieces of the jigsaw fit together properly and will not let you down with a bump in the middle of the night. It is unlikely at this stage that gas appliances will be working, for few vehicles are offered for sale complete with gas bottles, but now is the time to check electrical devices such as fluorescent lamps and the water pump. If the latter whirrs but produces no water at the faucet, switch off. There is probably no water in the container and pumps that are run dry soon expire for good. Remember to pull all the curtains, to ensure that they do their job adequately and, finally, sit down again and note any interior signs of damage that you think should be rectified before sale.

If your list of faults is not by now half as long as your arm, you are probably on to a winner. In any case, make a copy of it and retire to the sales office, having decided whether you want the motorcaravan or not.

If it has fallen far short of your expectations, say so and leave a copy of your list as you depart. If you have decided you would like it, the list can be used in one of two ways. Either you want the faults put right or you will take the brute with all its failings (except any which could make it dangerous) at a reduced price. Whichever is agreed, ensure that there is no misunderstanding about what is or is not to be done, preferably with written confirmation incorporated into any sales agreement which you sign. (Most firms will offer a carbon or photocopy for your retention and must do so if hire purchase is involved.) There should also be an understanding about what equipment, if any, will be removed from your existing vehicle offered in part exchange.

Before returning at a pre-arranged time to complete the transaction and take over the new motorcaravan, it is advisable to telephone to confirm that it will be ready and have all systems functioning. If you are not known to them, it is quite usual for dealers to ask for any payments by cheque to be made in advance, to allow time for clearance. If you do not know the dealer all that well, or are not convinced that he will honour all his obligations by the due date, offer to arrive with a banker's draft instead.

Take a gas bottle with you, if one is not to be supplied with the new motorcaravan. Install it and check that the gas appliances are working. Using your copy of the list, run over all the things that should have been done, and have a quick look over the exterior to ensure that no scrapes have been sustained since your last inspection. If everything is not as it should be, you can either swallow your impatience and say you will come back later to collect, when the work agreed has been carried out, or accept the vehicle then and there on the firm understanding that it will be returned, on an agreed date, for the work to be completed. Then you can hand over the banker's draft and your old vehicle.

It is unlikely that you will be given the registration document at this stage. I find that most dealers send it off themselves for transfer of ownership to be recorded and the road tax will have been included in the settlement figure. Most dealers also say they will take the document for the old vehicle as it is and notify the authorities. I have heard of cases of their neglecting to do so. It is your responsibility.

Many insurance policies now cover the holder for any one vehicle and the certificate may not bear a registration number. Your new vehicle will therefore be insured, in law, but for third party risks only. Notify the insurers immediately of the substitution. If you belong to a club, you may have been asked to say what vehicle you owned. They, too, should then be notified.

Legal aspects of buying

Motorcaravan dealers are usually friendly and trustworthy folk, so why the horrifying list of precautions on the last few pages? The vast majority would, it is true, put right any defects discovered within a reasonable time as a matter of goodwill. If you come to a firm understanding about where responsibilities lie, there is less chance of any misunderstanding cropping up later.

Like all motoring editors, I have had complaints from readers about the service offered by some advertisers. Some have been justified and were attended to immediately once one of the principals was informed. A few complaints were frivolous and a number the fault of the owner—like the one who drove a new vehicle a couple of hundred miles with the oil-pressure warning lamp glowing and then demanded a new engine. When satisfaction for a legitimate complaint cannot be obtained, I advise the unfortunate owner to resort to the legal departments of the AA, RAC or Consumers' Association or, when appropriate, the County Court. A book, *How to Sue in the County Court*, can be obtained from the Consumers' Association. It is a moderately simple DIY operation. Other sources of advice include the Citizens' Advice Bureau, Trading Standards Officer or Weights and Measures department (the latter for disputes about odometer readings). If you think that you may, unfortunately, be involved in a dispute with a dealer, keep copies of all correspondence and make notes about any telephone or personal conversations. Manufacturers of motorcaravans will sometimes accept responsibility or act on your behalf although they are in law not obliged to do so, except in the case of a direct sale, when the manufacturer is also the retailer.

Whereas a defect on a new base vehicle should be attended to under guarantee by any franchised repairer for the make, the same is not, in general, true for the caravan part of the outfit. There just are not sufficient motorcaravans around, although a manufacturer who admits a fault in his product will sometimes authorise rectification by one of his authorised dealers. But, in the end, the customer's channel for any complaint, be it on vehicle or caravan, is the person who sold it to him—which is why I would think three times before buying privately.

Private sales do not receive the same protection in law as those through a trader. Be especially wary of buying from traders who pretend they are private individuals. They are usually doing it to escape their legal obligations. You have also got to be certain that there are no outstanding hire purchase debts. For further advice on this and all other aspects of buying (and selling) see *The Consumer and the Law* and other publications of the Consumers' Association.

The Consumers' Association also take a long, hard look from time to time (in *Which?* and *Money Which?*) at ways of borrowing money for vehicle purchase. A bank overdraft is usually by far the cheapest but is seldom available over more than a few months. It is worth having a chat with your bank manager, who will probably suggest a personal loan, which should bear less interest than a hire-purchase agreement. It is impractical to lay down firm guidelines here, however, because the picture can change from month to month. There is no alternative to doing your own research on the spot, as I discovered when asking my own bank for a personal loan. At the time, they had used up their monthly allocation and recommended an associated finance house. This was bad advice, for my local motorcaravan dealer was able to obtain a lower interest rate from a small hire-purchase company whose rates beat those of any finance house.

If you have a mind to do so, it is worth studying the law on such matters. If the purchase is made outright, with borrowed money, the lender has no liabilities. A hire-purchase company does, however, bear some liability for the goods being fit for the purpose for which they were bought.

Selling

So much for buying. Selling is a different matter. Motorcaravan dealers expect a hefty mark-up which seems excessive until you examine all the facts. Dealers have many hidden expenses, which include value added tax on each sale, rent, rates, staff and interest on borrowed money—and most businesses seem to run on borrowed money these days. There are also bad debts. In the final analysis, the customer has to pay for the lot.

So it is sometimes better to sell privately, if you can stand the inconvenience and aggravation. It becomes a little depressing after the fifth potential customer, who has monopolised an hour or more of your time, goes away promising to return and then is never heard of again. But it is only fair to admit that many private agreements are concluded amicably and satisfactorily, to the mutual advantage of both parties, who arrive at a figure somewhere between what a dealer would pay and what he would charge. The continuing success of private deals is emphasised by the growing number of small ads in the specialist press and the never-to-be-ignored weekly, *Exchange & Mart*.

An alternative to the simple, straightforward but costly part exchange is sale on commission, which most dealers who sell you a vehicle would be happy to undertake. In brief, the motorcaravan remains your property but is displayed on the showground along with all other stock. The dealer will demonstrate it just like his own stock and, if you are lucky, will soon sell it, subtract his agreed commission (which will be less than his normal mark-up) and pay you the balance. Until sold, the vehicle is your property and it is essential to have a clear understanding, preferably in writing, of where responsibilities begin and end. The tax disc, for instance, may be surrendered and any balance due claimed, for insurance for demonstration purposes can be covered by trade plates. Your insurance may need to cater for fire, theft and vandalism.

Many motorcaravanners have used this sytem with complete satisfaction and dealers like it because their expensive capital is not tied up. But there are drawbacks. Your capital is idle, invested in a vehicle which you cannot use. Dealers have been known to go out of business overnight and all stock has 'disappeared'. This is fortunately extremely rare. Although the vehicle remains your responsibility, you are not in direct charge of it. If the vehicle is the subject of a hire-purchase agreement it is not yours, anyway, and permission of the financiers must be obtained.

Direct sale to a dealer is another possibility, especially if your motorcaravan is in good condition, of recent make or in short supply. You will not get as much for it as you would on part exchange, unless you are very lucky or the dealer has a customer waiting for such a vehicle. I have never known a dealer's cheque to bounce but have heard of the odd instance from a third party.

I am sometimes asked, in my capacity as an editor, to value a reader's motorcaravan—a chore I always refuse. If I had the time, my method would be to study the prices being asked in advertisements and tote the vehicle around to a few dealers for their opinion; a simple task easily undertaken by the owner. As motorists know, there is a confidential monthly publication called *Glass's Guide*, to which all dealers will refer. It is only a guide, not a bible, and if you were able to obtain a copy, it would not tell you how much you would get for your possession. Prices vary with supply and demand and geographical location.

All things considered, the popular part-exchange deal is the most convenient, if the most expensive. It is worth something simply to drive in with one vehicle and away with another. Most motorcaravan dealers will accept cars and even trailer caravans in part exchange—a point worth remembering if you are about to change your life style and become a motorcaravanner for the first time.

6
DIY — or not?

Having looked at new motorcaravans and staggered back at the prices being charged, you may be tempted, as I was in the early sixties, to buy a commercial van and build one yourself. Your determination may be reinforced when you have studied the prices of new commercial vans. Why, you will wonder, should a few sticks of furniture double the price?

Commercial vehicle prices are quoted excluding VAT, which must be paid anyway. Add to that the cost of everything that has to be done, then slap on car tax and more VAT, plus a reasonable profit margin, and you will soon arrive at a figure similar to that quoted by motorcaravan manufacturers.

There is no doubt, however, that you can save money by doing it all yourself, the biggest saving being on your own labour, for which you will presumably not charge yourself, though the tax man can levy VAT on it. You will end up with a motorcaravan which will have an unknown market value because it does not bear a recognised name tag. Dealers often lose interest when you try to sell or part exchange a 'private conversion'. Unless you are skilled in several crafts, it is a job best left to the experts.

You will meet frustration at every stage. Timber of a suitable grade is almost impossible to obtain locally in small quantities. Little things like cupboard catches will have you scouring the DIY shops for miles around. Special tools will be needed for cutting apertures for roof and windows and, in doing so, there is a chance of weakening the structure of the vehicle to such an extent that it could prove to be dangerous on the road, both to yourself and others.

Nevertheless, people continue to build their own motorcaravans and, knowing that the confirmed DIY addict will never be discouraged, I will do my best to point him in the right direction. But, before touching on complete conversions of vans to motorcaravans, let us have a look at the alternatives which will satisfy the creative passions of all but the most determined and probably prove to be safer and more saleable.

The easy way, and the one I now favour after many years of trial

Surely a one-and-only DIY exercise: coachbuilt body on a Rover 3 litre

and error, is to buy a motorcaravan that is nearly right for one's purposes and spend time and money in making it wholly suitable. It is impossible to enumerate the thousand-and-one small improvements that can be carried out on even the most expensive manufactured motorcaravans but you will pick up lots of ideas and 'how-tos' in the specialist magazines.

You can do quite a lot in the way of modification to make a small space more convenient to live in—altering the way a door hangs, for instance, or dividing it into two so that it occupies less room when opened. Stick-on clothes hooks in strategic places can be a boon, so is a mirror that can actually be used. Mirrors should always be stuck down and screwed. Your family will not appreciate bits of jagged glass flying around in a minor shunt. Perspex mirrors are becoming available but you have to search for them.

Provided you confine your DIY efforts to minor modifications, you can still justly claim, when selling, that it is the original model.

Should you go so far as rearranging all the furniture into an entirely different layout, you would at least have to describe it as 'modified' and might find that a dealer would not want it anyway.

There are certain safety requirements that must be observed when making major alterations and the most important will be dealt with in the succeeding pages.

Converting

People often ask me to recommend a book about conversion of a van. I do not think there is one, although the Motor Caravanners' Club can supply a duplicated manual which will answer many questions. It is revised periodically and should be reasonably up to date. Plans, with scaled cutting diagrams for furniture to fit the older vans, are available from the Auto Camping Club.

The average DIY enthusiast without special cabinet-making and coachbuilding skills should look carefully at the various kits available from established manufacturers—a system pioneered by Richard Holdsworth and since taken up by others. Many such people offer a complete conversion service and you can avail yourself of as much or as little as suits your pocket and inclination. You can drive a van to the factory (by appointment) and load it with items of furniture, equipment and windows, perhaps even strapping a rising roof kit on top. You take the lot away and assemble it at leisure during weekends and holidays. It is also possible to have KD (knock-down) kits sent by carrier.

It is worth having the difficult bits done for you at the factory. Windows and a rising roof or high top can usually be installed by the professionals in one day. The interior lining of the roof and trimming of the bare metal panels at the top of the van is a fairly skilled operation and one best left to the experts. You will find your creative instincts are amply exercised below roof level assembling and fitting all the furniture and perhaps incorporating your own modifications and improvements as you progress. If you follow the instructions and standard layout closely and take pains to achieve a nice finish (at least three coats of varnish), your motorcaravan will be indistinguishable from one built at the factory. As a result, it will be entitled to bear a recognised name tag and, when the time comes to sell, it will have a known market value.

If you are determined to do the whole lot yourself, you are

largely on your own and will therefore need a background of all the necessary skills. Should you need a book or instruction manual to tell you what to do and how to do it, then this complete DIY exercise is not advisable. The following notes therefore contain some pointers, intended as reminders for the initiated rather than instructions for complete amateurs.

The first golden rule when converting a van is to build back more strength than you take out. The top and sides of a metal body are not there just to keep the weather out; they are part of the integral structure and removing large parts of them will seriously weaken the whole vehicle. Remembering this, never drive a van between cutting the apertures and fitting windows or the roof. Vehicle manufacturers will often advise what may or may not be removed or altered, though some will say 'don't' to any modifications. You need body-shop experience to decide for yourself which roof bows or side pillars are structural or merely there to prevent vibration.

Only the most ambitious will consider building their own roofs or making window frames. These items are usually bought-in and should be accompanied by templates. Check them, to see that the

An old Bedford van made into something rather special, spotted at a motorcaravan fair

right ones have been supplied, then stick them to the roof or walls of the van with a water-soluble adhesive that can later be washed off.

There are several tools available for the cutting operation. Electric nibblers can be hired or attachments bought for drills. I used a Monodek sheet-metal cutter, hand operated. (There are several similar tools.) It was hard going but I was able to remove complete panels for use elsewhere. With a nibbler you usually end up with a lot of curly bits of scrap metal. Unless instructions indicate otherwise, leave a small radius at each corner rather than cutting it square. The latter can lead to splits running from the corner. If, in spite of your best efforts, a split does occur, drill a small hole $\frac{1}{8}$in (3mm) or so at the end of the split to prevent it creeping further. The same technique, with perhaps a slightly larger hole, can sometimes be used to control cracks in timber, but it does not always work.

If you are determined to build your own roof, cut away as little as possible of the original van. In particular, leave the cant rail (the curved part above the guttering) in position. It can later be used to support cupboards or bed bases. Do not touch the cab roof at all. It is possible to buy, or have made up, an angle-iron framework, of about 1 × 1in (25 × 25mm), the size of the aperture. If this is done, cut the aperture smaller and swage up the excess sheet metal to fold around the angle iron, making small fillets to round off the square corners.

Believe it or not, most glass-fibre high tops are now stuck on; but I would suggest adding a few rustless bolts at strategic points for peace of mind. A line of rivets would serve but they look awful unless disguised with trim. It is much easier, by the way, to line a high top with foam-backed vinyl or carpet type material before it is mounted on the vehicle.

Windows will come with their own fixing devices, the simplest being a rubber channel of such a section as to slip over the edge of the aperture which has been cut. That is easy; getting the window glass in can be a problem. Lubricating the rubber with washing-up liquid or a jelly hand cleaner can help, as can a piece of string in the groove which is gradually pulled away as the glass is inserted. The

Contora double-glazed acrylic windows come in standard sizes

window supplier may be prepared to lend you a special tool. Here, four hands are better than two. Although the glass is toughened or laminated (by law), it will shatter if it receives a knock. An old foam mattress on the ground could avoid an expensive accident. If you are supplying your own glass, take paper templates to automobile glass suppliers (listed in Yellow Pages), not the local glass merchant. Ask for edges to be polished and be prepared to wait for the order to be completed.

Remember to coat with paint any bare edges of metal, or holes that have been drilled, before covering them. Windows and roof completed, now is the time to start on the inside.

The simplest way to treat the floor is to cover the whole lot with $\frac{3}{4}$in (20mm) chipboard. Provided the sheets are large they will not need fastening down but a layer of thick felt between the van's metal floor and the false floor is recommended. Manufacturers tend to put the floor covering down at this stage, before installing furniture, because it makes for simplicity and avoids the need to cut awkward shapes around furniture units. Once down, however, it cannot be removed. The usual system is carpet in the sitting area, cushioned vinyl in working areas and toilet compartments. The deeper the cushion backing the less slippery it seems to be. Some owners prefer vinyl all over—certainly it is easier to clean. If you have planned well, holes can be cut for water and gas services at this stage.

Furniture is usually made of wood, with Formica or a similar laminate on horizontal working surfaces. The easiest and quickest way is to cut panels of decorated chipboard $\frac{5}{8}$in (15mm) thick or more or plywood at least $\frac{3}{8}$in (10mm), (thicker for large doors) and assemble them into boxes of the correct size. As it is not advisable, ever, to screw into the edge of either material, joining at corners is best done with a batten at each corner on the inside of the cabinet. There are also various corner fasteners in DIY shops which simplify the job. Furniture units will be fastened to the floor by the same method. Whether using chipboard or plywood, buy special chipboard screws or self-tappers. The latter will also go into metal; both have a deeper thread and hold more firmly than standard woodscrews.

Arguments continue about the conflicting merits of the two materials. Plywood is lighter but more expensive and unframed doors can warp. Marine-grade ply or 'waterproof' has superior water resisting qualities. Chipboard can gradually disintegrate if water seeps into an edge—a common hazard because edges stand on floors. If chipboard is used, choose one with a real wood veneer. The cheaper 'printed' surface is difficult to touch up when damaged. Visible edges of chipboard can be covered simply with an iron-on edging strip. Both materials look better and last longer if framed with timber edging (around each panel or just doors and drawers). Suitable mouldings, plain or fancy to suit your taste, will be stocked by DIY shops.

Some DIY motorcaravanners develop an obsession for saving weight in the search for fuel economy. They will make all panels of thin plywood glued to a light wooden framework. Doors will need to be clad on both sides. Aluminium angle and square tube can be used for the same reason. Such weight saving exercises are essential if a little lightweight van is being converted.

Whether you make your own upholstery or order it to be made to measure will depend upon the skills available in the family. Latex foam is superior to the plastic type, but most individuals and professional converters use the latter because it is cheaper. Do remember that it is flammable, as are many of the modern materials used as covers. Foam can be cut to shape very easily with an electric carving knife and joined fairly easily with flooring adhesive. If you make covers, cut them oversize and button deeply for a professional appearance.

Installing standard equipment is no more difficult than similar operations in the house, provided several special safety rules are observed. Everything must be securely fastened down and the heavier it is the stronger the fixings must be. Flying ovens and refrigerators would make a crunch extremely unpleasant. Gas and water pipes and electric cables must be clipped at intervals, for they will have to stand up to vibration.

Plumbing

Plumbing is probably the easiest part because it is usually carried out in $\frac{1}{2}$in (12mm) bore plastic hose (specify non-toxic—not garden hose) for water supplies and $\frac{3}{4}$in (19mm) for waste from basin and sink. (Only very large motorhomes are likely to have a sewage holding tank and the suppliers of the marine type WC pan will provide purpose-made plumbing kits.) If you are skilled in domestic plumbing, it is worth considering installing that in the motorcaravan, for it will give less trouble in the long run. In any case, I would advise buying a small domestic sink, with $1\frac{1}{4}$in (30mm) waste outlet, rather than the standard caravan model with $\frac{3}{4}$in (19mm) waste which, with couplings, is reduced to $\frac{1}{2}$in (12mm) bore at critical points and is consequently subject to frequent blockages.

If an underfloor fresh-water tank is to be installed, it should be slung securely in a cradle bolted to the chassis or through the floor, using extremely large washers to spread the load, for each gallon of water weighs 10lb. Ensure there is no free movement and support the whole of the base of the tank with a sheet of $\frac{1}{2}$in (12mm) waterproof ply, preferably varnished or treated with preservative for extra protection. If it is anywhere near the exhaust pipe, provide a shield of non-flammable insulating material.

Fitting a filler cap will entail running a hose, usually about $1\frac{1}{2}$in (35mm) diameter, from the filler to the tank. As this could involve cutting a hole in the side of the van, consider running the hose from a convenient point in the engine compartment, where looks are not important. Label the orifice 'drinking water' in the language of all countries likely to be visited. Many manufacturers now fit water tanks within the body, often in a seat locker. It is much easier that way and will give a small measure of protection from frost but valuable storage space is lost. If the inboard tank leaks, it is a minor disaster. An alternative is to carry water porters in a cupboard (one will be needed for tank filling, anyway). A length of $\frac{1}{2}$in (12mm) hose is run from the tank to the pump. If the latter, whether manual or electric, is above the level of the tank, make sure it is self-priming and capable of raising water from below. An in-line gauze filter should be fitted between tank and pump.

An electric submersible pump is the simplest of all to fit and usually the quietest in operation. The pump is connected to one end of the hose and placed, with its cable, in the water container. The other end of the hose goes straight to a faucet and the cable, via a switch, to a 12V outlet. If two faucets are required (eg for sink and hand basin) they can be fed by the one pump via a 'T' or 'Y' branch but must have shut-off valves incorporated. A pressure-operated switch must be installed in the water line near the pump. Some pumps have them incorporated.

Hot-water systems can also be fed by the same pump but

detailed fitting instructions vary with each make. If you buy a water heater, check that instructions come with it. Pressure requirements are particularly critical with multi-outlet instantaneous heaters, whereas storage heaters are not usually so demanding.

I always use an in-line water filter/purifier, which is changed yearly, and have never suffered from bad tasting cups of tea. If the water takes a long time to gush out of the faucet after switching on or operating the pump, a non-return valve will hold it in the pipes and stop it draining back to the tank. If clear plastic hose is used, algae will grow within unless daylight is excluded. This can be done simply by wrapping the pipes with insulating or carpet tape. For the same reason, a black polythene tank is the best type to sling beneath the vehicle.

A 12V water-level gauge is simple to fit. It usually involves inserting a couple of probes into the side of a plastic tank (a job that can be done from the outside) and a little electric wiring. It is useful to have one on the waste-water tank, too. One gauge, with a change-over switch, may be used for both or any number of tanks.

Problems with a simple water system are fairly rare and electric pumps now seem very reliable and virtually maintenance free. Manual pumps (hand or foot operated) will need new washers occasionally. If water trickles rather than gushes out at the faucet, check that all joints are securely fastened with hose clips and that there are no kinks in the hoses. A water hose which follows a gentle curve in cold weather can develop a kink when the weather warms up. It is best to cut the hose at the kink and install an elbow but a 'spring' can be made from rustless wire (brass or copper, not galvanised) and inserted in the pipe at the offending place. If pressure still remains low, disconnect the supply pipe from the outlet at the tank and check that the outlet hole is clear by poking with wire. A hole that is too small can be drilled out carefully, preferably with a twist drill in a hand-operated wheel brace so that you can 'feel' your way and avoid penetrating the sidewall.

There is a new plumbing system called 'Qest' for hot- and cold-water systems in caravans. It uses compression fittings and non-kink opaque flexible hoses and is well-worth considering for the more ambitious hot and cold installations. It would be particularly appropriate for heat-exchanger systems which use waste heat

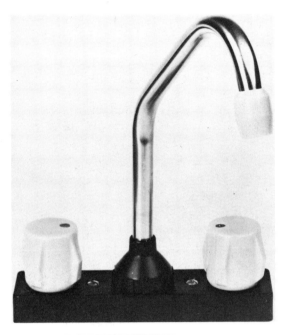

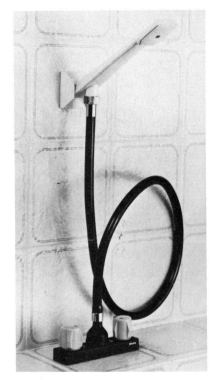

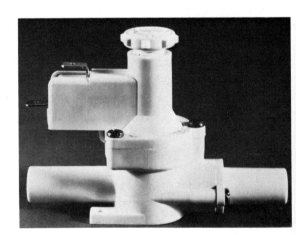

Water taps for caravans by Whale Pumps

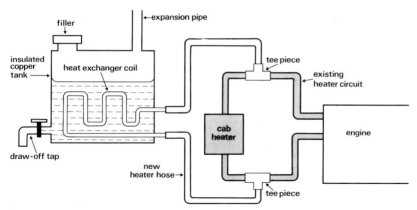

Diagrammatic view of heat exchanger hot water system. Draw-off tap may be connected to the plumbing system of the caravan via a pump

from the engine's cooling circuit to supply a tank full of 'free' hot water when motoring.

Complete heat-exchanger hot-water tanks can be bought. A competent plumber could make one. It consists of a 5–6 gal (22–27 litre) tank with a copper pipe coiled inside, which is teed-in to the flow and return of the vehicle's heater hoses. Water reaches near boiling temperature within a few miles of motoring and, with an insulated tank, will remain warm overnight. It can be drawn off direct from the tank, by gravity, or pumped to one or more supply points, using an electric pump. I have found that the very hot water soon softens the washers on hand pumps. Using two electric pumps—one each for hot and cold supplies—it is a simple plumbing job to feed a shower head via a mixer control or two separate and adjustable cocks. Polythene hose will withstand hot water for a time but it is better to use copper pipe or Qest.

Instantaneous and storage water heaters are also designed to supply showers. A very simple shower can, however, be rigged up using a 'pump-up' garden insecticide spray. It is surprising how wet you can get standing in a large bowl with a gallon or so of water delivered through a fine spray head. This 'shower' system has the advantage that it can be used outside as a 'refresher' or in a toilet tent. Complete kits are on the market, but here we are leaving the realms of DIY.

Waste water from the sink can be allowed to run into a bucket beneath the vehicle, or two buckets if there is a sink and wash basin. I am a great advocate of the fitted waste-water tank for it allows full use of the motorcaravan in any situation. At its simplest, the tank can be a collapsible plastic container at the end of the waste pipe, stored in the bottom of a cupboard, but most waste tanks are of black polythene and fastened beneath the floor. Follow the same mounting precautions as applied to fresh-water tanks. The ridiculously small outlets from standard caravan sinks, already mentioned, encourage water to dribble rather than pour down the waste pipe. It helps if the sink has an overflow outlet, when water seems to run more freely. The same effect can be achieved if two sinks, or a sink and hand basin, are mounted close to each other and teed-in to a common waste pipe as high up as possible. It seems useless to join them low down, near the tank.

A shower tray poses a small problem. It is possible for waste water from sink or basin to enter through the plug hole, though it will all drain eventually into the waste tank. Careful planning of the waste plumbing runs is necessary—or there must be two inlets into the common waste tank.

You may, if you wish, buy expensive non-toxic polythene hose for the waste pipes. But there is a much cheaper corrugated hose available at accessory shops. It can be taken round fairly sharp bends without kinking but, for maximum flow, should be run as near straight as possible.

Filling a large water tank with portable carriers is quite a chore, especially if the filler orifice is sited fairly high. Roll-flat hoses take up very little room and are a boon, for you need only drive somewhere near a water tap rather than right up to it. The hose must be labelled 'non-toxic'. An alternative to the lifting of water porters is to stand them on the ground and use a submersible pump and a short length of hose to raise the water for you. The submersible pump can be powered via cable and crocodile clips on to the vehicle's battery but a neater solution is to install a filler orifice which incorporates a 12V socket and a lockable cap. Accessory shops have them.

Electrics

Electric wiring for these and all other appliances needs little specialised skill but must be done carefully. We all learnt at school that watts = volts × amps. Now the simple equation comes into its own in showing that low voltage currents (correctly, extra-low voltage) need thicker cables. For instance, $12W = 12V \times 1A$, $12W$ being about the consumption of one small fluorescent lamp. At mains voltages, $12W = 240V \times \frac{1}{20}A$. So a 12V cable needs to be 20 times as thick to operate the same appliance. Do remember to use grommets where electric cables run through holes in metal and make sure the cable cannot be pinched anywhere by subsequent furniture installation. It is advisable to keep a record of hidden cable runs, so that you do not later inadvertently drive a screw or nail through it. It will be cheaper to buy a reel of suitable cable (from an automobile electrical supplier) than measured lengths. The snag is that positive and negative will then be the same colour, so, wherever the cable is cut to take an appliance or enter a junction box, use coloured insulating tape for identification of polarity. This is the only time insulating tape should be used. All joints should be via screwed flex connectors, junction boxes or crimp connectors. The bars of plastic flex connectors available in DIY and accessory shops are suitable for low-voltage wiring to fluorescent lamps and water pumps, but not for cable carrying anything over about 5A. For mains current, use proper junction boxes. Every circuit should have a fuse of the correct rating, using line fuses or a fuse box. The equation (watts = volts × amps) will allow you to calculate fuse rating and cable capacity.

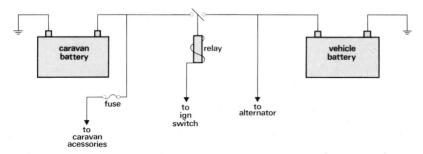

The basics of caravan electrics. A blocking diode may be used in place of relay. Detailed wiring instructions come with kits

Mains-electric hook-up points are becoming increasingly available at camp sites. An input of mains electricity is valuable when the vehicle is to remain stationary for some time, and avoids the need to run the engine to charge the batteries. A good vehicle battery will cope with demands from a water pump and fluorescent lamps overnight. If there are any further electrical demands, a second battery is advisable—one reserved for caravan services, so that the main battery retains enough punch to start the motor. A simple bit of arithmetic will indicate whether you are likely to need an extra supply of electricity. A small fluorescent lamp will be rated at 13W. Referring to the equation, watts = volts × amps, that means it will consume just over 1A on the usual 12V system. In theory, with a 56A/hour battery, you could run this one lamp for nearly 56 hours. In practice, leaving the lamp on continuously would exhaust the battery sooner than that, but it is a rough guide. The current demanded for starting the vehicle next morning is pretty terrific and, in practice, it is advisable to have 20 or more amp/hours available, depending to a large extent on weather, humidity and the eccentricities of your vehicle (some fire immediately, others always demand a spot of starter flogging). If you are running a television (especially colour), extractor fan or blown-air spaceheater, two batteries are advisable, even for one night's sojourn.

There is not enough space here to delve into all the intricacies of wiring for two batteries, but the basics can be covered. In essence, there are three methods (each with several subdivisions): (a) automatic; (b) manual; and (c) permanent connection. We will take them in reverse order.

(c) Simplest is to double the battery capacity by connecting like terminals of both batteries. There are snags. Wiring must be heavy enough to take starter current. Look at the cable running from the vehicle's battery to the starter solenoid to ascertain the necessary gauge. If one battery fails, the good one will feed it until both are exhausted. Over-enthusiastic use of caravan facilities could flatten both batteries.

(b) A simple switching system can be arranged to disconnect the second (caravan) battery from the primary (vehicle) battery when starting the motor and when camping. A suitable heavy duty switch can be obtained from marine chandlers. Snag: you are relying upon memory, although the DIY enthusiast could devise a system of warning lights.

(a) An automatic system will do the thinking for you, isolating the caravan battery when parked, charging it from the vehicle's generator when motoring. It sounds marvellous but I regret to say that, as an editor, I have had so many complaints from readers that

I have lost confidence in the various systems. Many provide only a trickle charge to the second battery, others have been the subject of all sorts of failings. One I had fitted (by a qualified automobile electrician) drained the car's battery completely and left the secondary untouched. Another demanded over 100 miles of motoring to put back enough current to work just the fluorescent lamps.

As a compromise I have adopted a semi-manual system. A power pack, as sold for trailer caravans, consists of a battery and packet of electronic wizardry in a convenient portable box. Plugged into any 12V socket, the caravan battery is charged. The power pack can also be plugged into the mains for charging, so it is useful in the house too. If the 12V socket is controlled by the ignition key, the power pack is isolated when you are not motoring. The power pack can also take advantage of mains electricity on site and all the 12V equipment can be run to your heart's content, when the battery becomes merely a 'smoother', evening-out any mains fluctuations.

As more and more campsites offer mains electricity, for the majority of motorhomes which are equipped to take it, the private converter may be tempted to wire his own motorcaravan. My advice here is not necessary. If he is a qualified electrician, he will know how. If he is not, he should seek the services of one. The combination of a metal van, wet grass and a frayed cable can be lethal — and the fault need not be in your own vehicle, but in a neighbour's outfit or the site's wiring. Unlike gas, electricity does not announce the fact that it is leaking.

Gas

Gas plumbing, on the other hand, can be undertaken with a few tools, a little knowledge and a fair degree of patience. Do not be tempted to take the easy way out and run a length of flexible hose from the gas container to the appliance. And do not use any rubber hose at all. The correct product is neoprene, available from bottled gas suppliers. Even that perishes, and should be renewed every few years.

To begin at the beginning: the gas containers (bottles or cylinders) should be secured in a locker of their own, ventilated downwards via a hole of about $1\frac{1}{2}$in (38mm) diameter to the exterior. Ideally, the gas locker should be metal lined and accessible only from the exterior of the vehicle. The latter has its snags, because people get lazy about going outside to turn off the gas. The regulator on the bottle—which with butane reduces pressure to about 11in (28mbar) on a water gauge, and with propane to 14in (37mbar)—should be connected to the caravan's plumbing system by a short but adequate length of neoprene tubing, secured with a hose clip at each end. As close as possible to the bottle, but inside the caravan and easily accessible, there should be a main shut-off cock, or bank of cocks if there is more than one gas appliance.

Gas plumbing in caravans is usually carried out in $\frac{1}{4}$in copper pipe. Do not worry about metrication here. Every supplier will know what you mean by $\frac{1}{4}$in copper piping—and could gape open mouthed if you spoke metric. The copper pipe is easily bent in the hand but should not be taken around a radius of less than about 2in (5cm), when buckling may occur. It is advisable to bend it round a former—anything solid and of the right curvature. Most professionals will bend and cut a length of pipe to shape, offering it up to the job time after time, before fixing it to the couplings at each end.

Joints are simplicity itself, using compression fittings. The pipe is cut with a hacksaw at right angles and any burr removed with a file. The coupling (cock, tap, elbow or whatever) will come with nut and olive (the latter, before use, will look like a short piece of pipe, just large enough to slip over your $\frac{1}{4}$in pipe). Remove nut and olive and thread on to the end of the gas pipe. Push the latter as far as it will go into the coupling. Doing up the nut will squeeze the olive into shape and result in a gastight joint. There should be no need to use any joint sealer but, if you have made a hash of things, a blob of 'Calortite' or short length of PTFE (polytetra-fluoroethylene) tape, from gas suppliers, may get you out of trouble. You can buy a leak tester at accessory shops—worthwhile if you have done a lot of gas plumbing. Alternatively, a bottled-gas installer will test your rig for you. The human nose is a very good tester, too, for a revolting smell has been added to the odourless liquefied petroleum gas (LPG) to warn of any leaks.

Gas plumbing is easy and the complete novice will gain confidence and expertise after making the first joint. Practice makes perfect, so buy a few spare olives and an extra length of pipe to make mistakes on. Cleanliness is essential. A bit of grit will ruin

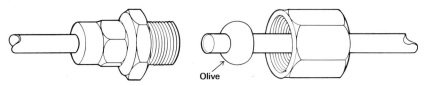

Making a joint in ¼in copper gas pipe. Two spanners are needed. The olive assumes the shape shown after the joint is made

a joint and dust in pipes will clog jets. Pipes should run straight to joints, not at an angle, and any curves necessary should be formed before making the joints. Nuts should not be overtightened — gentle pressure on the spanner is all that is needed. Pipe runs should be clipped at intervals to prevent sagging and vibration. This is particularly important if any work is carried out beneath the floor.

Finally, the usual caution must be added: never search for a gas leak with a match. Use soapy water or a special spray-on detector sold by gas suppliers. Before using your DIY gas installation for the first time it is advisable to have it tested professionally.

Other possibilities

I have said nothing about constructing a coachbuilt body on a chassis-cab because this is hardly a job for an amateur; nor is it advisable to try to mount a trailer-caravan body on to a four-wheeled vehicle. The average lightweight caravan would fall apart, according to the makers of the latter. But there are several attractive box bodies on the commercial market, some of which form the basis for minibuses. They sell secondhand at reasonable prices and offer interesting possibilities to the competent DIY enthusiast. It is advisable to consult the makers of the body about what is safe to do. Some are deliberately lightweight and of flimsy construction, to keep the commercial van out of the heavy goods league. Adding a roof rack could, for instance, result in alarming distortion due to parallelogramming and eventual total collapse — and an embarrassing court appearance for the owner. Coaches and buses offer tremendous scope for those prepared to drive and store them, and windows and headroom are already provided. Be warned, though: some campsites and clubs will not accept them.

Tax on conversions

Of course, the tax man will want his cut. You will have to pay

VAT on any commercial van you buy and on the equipment to go in it. There will also be an obligation to pay car tax, which will vary according to the age of the vehicle and the amount of equipment put into it. The address of the local officer of Customs and Excise will be in the telephone directory. Have a chat with him before starting. He will tell you all the answers and give some idea of how much (if anything) will be charged as a 'notional amount' on your own spare time labour. There are other people who must be informed about the change of use applying to the vehicle. The Driver and Vehicle Licensing Authority at Swansea will want to know, so that the registration document can be altered. Your insurers must also be informed. They may require an engineer's certificate and will put you in touch with the appropriate person. Perhaps now, the reasons for sticking to modifications to an existing motorcaravan will be clear. Once the tax has been paid, there is no further charge, however ambitious the improvements.

Safety

I am a great believer in seat belts. Front seats will have them anyway and rear seats should. Again, this is not a DIY exercise for those who do not know how to set about it but you might, at planning stage, arrange furniture so that harnesses can later be installed professionally. Ask a main dealer in your make of vehicle about possible rear attachment points.

Safety must be the prime consideration of every DIY constructor. Regulations are inevitably going to become more stringent regarding both commercial and private conversions, but in the end it is the user's responsibility to ensure that he exposes neither himself, family nor other people to any avoidable hazard. In particular:

Build in more strength than you take out.

Construct and fasten everything firmly.

Avoid dangerous projections and sharp edges.

Allow clear access to exits at all times.

Check gas and electric installations frequently.

Use only safety glass (acrylic sheet is permissible on windows to the rear of the driving compartment).

Avoid large mirrors; stick and screw all mirrors.

Put a fuse in every electric circuit.

Incorporate adequate permanent ventilation that cannot be closed.

Carry a fire extinguisher and fire blanket by the cooker.

Do not attempt DIY conversions beyond your capabilities.

My conversion mistakes

In an earlier chapter I promised mention of my own DIY activities which began with that under-powered Standard Atlas van, bought new for less than £500 (so it was some time ago). I hope a few readers will profit from my mistakes.

The family took a hand at the planning stage. As we were all impatient to complete the project and head for the open road, a simple layout was chosen, with a centre gangway and beds along each wall, to be used as daytime settees. The child's bunk was made up in the cab. This left just enough room in the rear corners for a cooker on one side and sink on the other.

Looking at all the space available in the empty van, I was not bothered (then) about space-saving equipment. So the cooker was powered by a big 32lb (15kg) gas container, which occupied all the space beneath. The cupboard below the sink held a large, metal Elsan chemical closet. It had to be emptied each time we moved for it had no sealing lid (it was put to its designed purpose in a canvas shelter attached to the rear door). Water was carried in a container which got in everyone's way, because it had no home. There was no cupboard storage space. Everything had to go in the lockers beneath the seats. At virtually every meal time, something had been forgotten when setting the table, so it was a case of 'all out', whilst the mattresses were shifted and the lids lifted. And they were heavy, cumbersome, spring interior mattresses—because we did not know any better.

There was no rising roof. The van's bare metal was lined with plywood, with glass wool as insulation. It was an awful job bending the plywood to follow (approximately) the curve of the roof.

Fluorescent lamps were unknown. There was one miserable gas lamp, and the mantle had to be removed when travelling to stop it shaking itself to pieces.

We quarrelled during the first holiday but stuck it out and explored a lot of England and Wales, venturing into Snowdonia. Unexpectedly, the Atlas coped manfully with all the hills. We drove along Britain's then only stretch of motorway—just 6 miles of it around Preston—and were carried on the fantastic Victorian transporter bridge between Runcorn and Widnes now, like trams and steam trains, long gone.

We learnt a lot from the mistakes made in the Atlas, but not enough, for more were to come with its successor, an Austin 152. It was chosen because it possessed sliding doors which, with safety harnesses worn, could be opened whilst motoring. Delightful—but I had ignored the fact that the doors slid backwards on the inside of the vehicle and consequently reduced the van's interior width by six inches or more. So we could not adopt what was then becoming the conventional layout of transverse settee-double bed behind the cab. The kitchen was located there, across the bulkhead. Single beds were again longitudinal, one each side, but this time they were constructed as a pair of single dinettes with wall-mounted table between, rather like a first-class Pullman dining car. This was an entirely successful feature and I am surprised it has not been adopted commercially.

We had learnt that a rising roof was highly desirable, so I made the cap of marine ply. It was heavy but looked smart provided the varnish was renewed frequently. It was, though, heavy to raise. After trying hinges on side, front and rear, I decided I wanted a permanent high top—and built one. It was strong, being curved from front to rear with flat sidewalls, and waterproof, but offered limited full standing room.

The registration, TOY, appropriately described our third vehicle, which was based upon a side valve, 1100cc, Ford Escort van. This little package contained all life-support systems, with four forward-facing passenger seats, kitchen and a chemical closet. Rear passenger seats were based on camping chairs, removable for use outside and clamped to the floor when travelling. They could be turned to face backwards when camping, when two little wall-mounted tables provided rudimentary dining facilities (there never was room for four at table). The chemical closet was carried as luggage and used in a tent extension on site.

This complete equipment in such a small van was made possible by ignoring a downstairs bed. The always-ready double was incorporated into a roof capsule, about 8ft (2.4m) long and spanning the full width from gutter to gutter. To obtain the necessary length, the roof extended a couple of feet beyond the

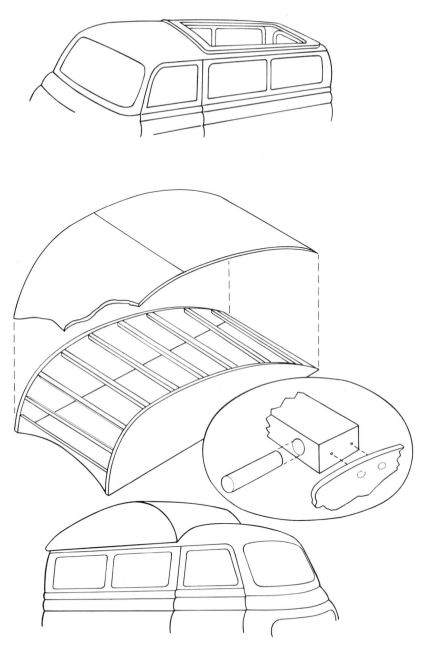

A strong but simple high top constructed from marine ply, as fitted to the author's Austin 152 some years ago. The hole cut in the van's roof must first be reinforced. Inset shows method of screwing into end grain of cross-bracers. Only for those with relevant woodworking experience windscreen. The rising roof was front hinged and occupants of the double bed therein slept with feet forward, climbing up to bed through a hatch in the rear. I thought the idea was terrific. My wife did not like it, because it took a long time to get into and out of bed. Although I provided a sharp knife upstairs to cut the canvas sidewalls in an emergency, she never was happy and TOY was sold for scrap.

After that, I concentrated on modifying existing motorcaravans, and continue to do so because no-one seems to be able to manufacture what I want at an affordable price.

7
Living in a motorcaravan

To get the greatest benefit from an expensive purchase, it is sensible to make full use of it all the year round. Properly equipped and used, it is so much more than a recreational vehicle. But for year-round use, a motorcaravan must be sensibly equipped, which is far different from filling it with a lot of useless gimmicks.

Heating

In winter, some form of heating will be essential. Camping shops sell little radiant heaters which screw directly to the top of a gas cylinder. Avoid them as if your life depended upon it—for it could. In a large tent or annexe it may be possible to avoid brushing against the thing. The small amount of free space in most motorcaravans increases the hazard to unacceptable proportions.

When really pushed, my wife and I used a catalytic heater screwed to a Camping Gaz bottle (as a temporary measure and when we knew there would be no children around). The catalytic heater has no flame and gives off no poisonous fumes, or only minute traces. I have seen petrol poured over one when it was alight. It merely evaporated—but it is not an experiment that should be conducted outside a laboratory. Clothes which brush against such a heater will not catch fire. But, if the heater is starved of oxygen, it begins to glow red and could then become dangerous. It consumes a great deal of oxygen. We discovered that a roof vent half open was insufficient and had to open a side window, too—not an easy decision with frost all around outside.

If a really well-guarded radiant heater could be found and screwed to a wall away from draughts (but still well ventilated), that might just be acceptable in a fairly spacious motorhome not overcrowded with people. I do not think the risk is acceptable with children, who have a habit of trying to squeeze past adults in confined spaces. But if the wall-mounted heater were catalytic instead of radiant, the risk would be reduced considerably, to more or less acceptable proportions. But the heater would still need copious supplies of fresh air. Small convector heaters with a 'batswing' flame are safer, but give out very little warmth.

None of the above mentioned appliances has a flue and, in addition to consuming large amounts of the oxygen essential to the human life in the caravan, give off considerable quantities of water vapour. It can be measured in pints or even gallons. Much of it condenses on any cold surface, wetting cushions, clothes and bedding. It is unfortunate that all the wrong sorts of heaters are also the cheapest to buy and easiest to install. While the cost of radiants and simple catalytics can be measured in £10s, the more desirable heaters will approach or be well into three figures.

·In a confined space, such as a converted van, an underfloor heater is an asset. Like most of the others in this section, it has a balanced flue, which means that you do not need a chimney through the roof. Air for combustion is drawn from the outside and expelled to the outside. The warm air that reaches the inside of the caravan is just pure, warm air, bearing no harmful products of combustion or added water vapour. It is lovely standing over the grille of an underfloor heater, allowing the warmth to filter up your legs. It is almost as pleasant standing in front of a wall-mounted balanced-flue heater. With these, the flue can be beneath the floor or, unobtrusively, in the side of the vehicle. Many are available with blown air as an optional extra, ensuring better circulation throughout the caravan. A thermostatic control is another desirable addition. With a properly planned gas system, all appliances except the heater can be turned off 'at the main'. Waking up cold during the night, it is a simple matter to flick the thermostat for a bit of warmth. Specify a heater with electric or piezo-electric ignition; if you do not you will have to climb out of bed and search for matches—or trust that the pilot light has not been blown out. (All but the very simplest heaters have flame failure devices, so there is no danger of unburnt gas reaching the interior.)

Balanced-flue heaters come in a variety of shapes and sizes. So do furnaces, a term borrowed from America. These rely on a fan both for circulation of warm air and exhaustion of products of combustion. The warm air will come out of a grille, or be ducted to a series of grilles around the vehicle. Imagine the joy of a warm

The Electrolux gas caravan heater is externally flued and can be fitted with a blown-air facility

toilet room on a cold morning. Another type of furnace stands upright in the wardrobe, with a flue going through the roof. It takes up little room, keeps clothes nicely aired, will even supply water-filled radiators anywhere in the caravan. For warmth in the rear when travelling, there is a radiator which runs from the vehicle's heater. Fitting is a simple matter but a few yards of reinforced car-heater hose will be needed. Apart from the conversions based on air-cooled Volkswagen buses (not vans) rear passengers in motorcaravans have seldom been able to benefit from engine heat.

I have not given names of heaters so far because there are very many models on the market and not all are easily available everywhere. But the next one will be named because it appears to be unique. The German Eberspächer runs from the vehicle's fuel tank—petrol or diesel. It is among the most expensive to buy but is cheap to run. It would consume about a gallon of fuel if left running continuously for a day and night but it punches out so much heat that it is difficult to imagine any situation in which that would be necessary. In a fairly small but poorly insulated motorcaravan, we found we needed it running for about 50 per cent of the time. A thermostat is available. A second battery to run the fan and glow plug (which ensures ignition) is desirable. In practice, we could detect no effect on the vehicle's fuel consumption and so considered that we were getting 'free' heating. It has the advantage of being small (about the size and shape of a metal hot-water bottle) so can be fitted almost anywhere. The Eberspächer may be used safely whilst motoring and could therefore provide a bit of comfort in older Volkswagens whose engines are tucked away at the back. New small gas heaters work like the Eberspächer but use less electricity.

Insulation

If you camp in cold weather, a heater will add only marginally to comfort if there is little or no insulation. Some van conversions are particularly lacking in this respect. Do not be fooled by attractive wall panels; there could be nothing but air between them and the metal skin. The beautiful covering beneath the GRP roof cap again could hide nothing but air. Older motorcaravans are the worst offenders and things are improving all the time.

There is a lot that the owner can do, or have done by one of the specialist firms offering improvements and modifications. Side panels can be removed (they are usually screwed into place) and felt packed behind. Felt will offer the additional advantage of noise reduction but lightweight expanded polystyrene is recommended for the roof. Use flame-retardant materials whenever available. Flexible walls to a rising roof pose a problem. Adding a layer of insulating material will make opening and closing difficult but I have seen quilted material hung in place after the roof was raised. It can be fastened with press studs or Velcro. The floor is easy: just a runner of carpet laid over whatever covering is there already. It can be taken out and brushed when necessary, which is useful in the muddy season.

If the caravan is short on space in the seating area, a few extra inches of room can be found in van conversions by discarding the side panels below the windows and sticking foam-backed carpet to the van's walls. Floor adhesive works well on painted metal. Cheap carpet bends more easily than good quality. Carpet is a reasonable insulator but, more important, its appearance and texture make one feel warm. For this reason, I am covering the sensible and washable walls of my present coachbuilt with carpet. It may begin to smell or look tatty after a few years. If it does, it will not take long to rip off and replace. I know one motorcaravanner who has lined the whole of the interior of his GRP-bodied Romahome with carpet. The improvement in cosiness is remarkable.

A lot of coldness strikes through windows. Insulating curtains or roller blinds can be bought in shops. Double glazing is an expensive option and not always available but it is possible to cut sheets of acrylic (glass substitute) to fix to the insides of windows during cold weather. They can be held in place with 'Stick-n-Stick' Velcro. Some winter wanderers use bulkier but lightweight sheets of expanded polystyrene placed against windows at night. I favour sheets of plywood covered with the same carpet as the walls, for a cosy feel. Solar control film has reflective properties and is claimed to prevent some heat loss. It is certainly effective during daytime in reducing heat build-up caused by the sun and adds a measure of privacy.

External, temporary 'double glazing' (a DIY job) consists of sheets of tough plastic, press-studded over windows when needed. It works very well, provided the window frame is so constructed

that there is a gap between glass and plastic. It is about the only system that can be used to 'double glaze' cab windows when parked. A special material has been developed for curved windscreens; a net is incorporated in the plastic sheet, to trap air between it and the glass. Double-glazed acrylic or glass windows are available to those building motorcaravans from scratch. The range of sizes is limited, so it is advisable to consult the window suppliers before finishing plans.

'Winterisation'

'Winterisation' calls for more than insulation and heating. The butane gas in general use fails to vaporise efficiently at below-zero temperatures. A kettle full of hot water poured over the gas bottle will often get it working—but where is the hot water to come from if you have no gas? Those with an Eberspächer heater can use its output of warm air, directed through a flexible hose (sold as an extra as a hair dryer). For the majority, the solution is to use propane gas in winter. It is more expensive and comes in bottles with different regulators but can be connected safely to standard gas systems. Do not risk buying bottle and regulator abroad. Caravans in some European countries work to a different pressure. It is safe to exchange the gas bottle overseas, provided the UK regulator is retained.

Water systems can be troublesome in freezing conditions and it is advisable to drain appliances such as water heaters. In theory, the complete plumbing system should be emptied, but you should at least ensure that tanks are not full, thus leaving room for the expansion which bursts frozen domestic pipes. Polythene tanks and hoses seem to cope with a bit of abuse. It is inadvisable to try to use electric water pumps when they are frozen. They will soon burn out. Carry a supply of water above floor level in a portable container, in the warmest spot in the caravan you can think of. A little portable camping stove with throwaway cartridges is a good idea—the theory being that you can go to bed with a cartridge to keep it warm and be assured of the morning cup of tea. (This is for occasions when you have not got around to substituting propane for the butane in the gas-bottle locker.)

Carpet trim does a lot towards insulation against both cold and noise

Camping in really cold weather, as when on a skiing holiday for instance, calls for very thorough preparation of vehicle, caravan and self. Warm clothing and thermal wear for sleeping are desirable and a great deal of body heat loss can be prevented by wearing a nightcap in bed. But real winter campers use sites equipped with mains-electric hookups for caravans. This is one occasion when it is not usual to try to be completely independent.

If snow falls in quantity, sweep it off the roof (for it weighs a lot) and keep ventilators clear (especially heater outlets, if you want to avoid possible asphyxiation). However cold the weather, ensure that there is some ventilation. In fact, a degree of ventilation is essential whenever the motorcaravan is occupied, whatever the weather.

Naturally, the vehicle should be fully serviced before setting off on a winter foray. Anti-freeze should be increased in strength if you are going somewhere really cold. Keep an eye on the coolant's temperature when motoring and, if necessary, blank off part of the radiator. Tyres must have plenty of tread and it is advisable to carry tyre chains. Some continental roads will be closed to vehicles without them but the majority of main roads will be cleared more efficiently than those in Britain. The tyre chains could come in useful at any time of the year, when getting out of muddy fields. However, it is not worth buying a set solely for that purpose. Accessory shops have various simple clamp-on devices for spinning wheels. There are also mats to put beneath the wheels. More about those and other accessories in Chapter 11.

Lifestyle

On the matter of food and drink it is not my intention to provide a set of ideal menus for the motorcaravanner. There are already books about caravan cooking. But do not get hooked on convenience foods. They have their place (kept in reserve, as 'iron rations'), but you are slumming if you rely on them too often. I suppose that indicates an attitude of mind. My wife and I agree that certain standards must be upheld when motorcaravanning. There is usually time to spare for a slower pace of life and a spot of more gracious living. We cannot afford top-class hotels but we can bring a little bit of luxury into motorcaravan holidays. Take coffee, for instance. We use the real stuff and enjoy the time-consuming ritual of making it, using filter papers. (These, incidentally, overcome the problem of disposing of the grounds.)

For entertainment, we take radio, tapes and a small television. The latter is seldom used, for the slower pace at which the day's routine is taken fills the time pleasantly. Evening 'sundowners', with conversation, are another ritual, and I have come to love the morning chores, pottering around emptying the waste tank and topping up the fresh water, checking the engine, while my wife does her pottering inside. So we enjoy motorcaravanning for its own sake. Any sights or excursions that occur are a bonus. The change from a fairly hectic working life is something to be anticipated with relish. Others will have different objectives.

Bed time is always a bit of a challenge. There are few motorcaravans in which one can just hop into bed as at home. There are cushions to be rearranged and blankets and sleeping bags to be sorted out. It can take up to half an hour, depending upon the number in the family. Most caravanners prefer sleeping bags because they are adaptable and can be really snug on a cold night. It is advisable to buy the most expensive you can afford. They will

Not 'convenience' food but very 'convenient' in hot weather if the refrigerator gives up

last for ages, anyway and those with synthetic fibres can be washed or dry cleaned. There are two things to look for: a draught seal on the zip and stitching that does not go right through from inside to outside. The latter will be found only on cheap bags; a lot of body heat can be lost if the inside and outside covering are stitched together, for there will be no insulation along the stitch lines. The size of the bag is a matter of personal preference; the weight should be fairly high. It is usually quoted in ounces: 38 is reasonable for general use, 44 desirable for really cold conditions. If the weather is warm, the zip can be undone, if hot, sleep on top of it or in the liner. (Liners are sheets sewn into a bag shape. Some people like them, others rely on frequent airing and regular washing or cleaning of the bag itself.) For extra warmth, we take a couple of car rugs and a pair of cellular blankets, the latter large enough to be used doubled if necessary. Then there is always the good old hot-water bottle. Pillows have covers which make them into cushions for daytime use.

Condensation beneath the bed is often a problem, for the body exudes water vapour as well as heat. Beds which employ a table as part of the base are particularly prone and though holes can be drilled in locker lids for ventilation it is not recommended on the table. A few layers of thick brown paper (unglazed), or even newspaper, will help. My own solution is to discard the table for bed support and bridge the gap with plywood boards, leaving a small gap between the boards. I have put folding legs on a couple of them; they make convenient little coffee tables, too. Brown paper finds another application in the upper stretcher bunks, where coldness can strike from beneath. The paper, spread beneath the bedclothes, will lessen this uncomfortable effect. A sheet of foam, if there is room to store it, will make them more comfortable.

Most of us pack far too many clothes for a holiday. In Britain, it is understandable, for we never know what the weather is going to do. In a motorcaravan's limited space it is therefore desirable to have garments that will serve more than one purpose. Sports shops offer attractive, lightweight yet warm outer clothing which, being fairly crease-resistant, can be bundled away anywhere, even folded into covers to make cushions. But the clothing that really decides the question of comfort is that worn next to the skin. If you have a set of thermal underwear for use when necessary, outer garments and rainwear can be lightweight, and so occupy less space in the wardrobe or clothes locker. If you want a 'best set' (perhaps for the occasional evening out) and the wardrobe is inadequate or non-existent, buy a folding wardrobe. They are often seen in mail-order advertisements, and can travel flat on a bed or stretcher, be hung up or bundled into the cab at night. In general though, clothes which will not suffer from rolling or folding are favourite.

Annexe tent or awning

You can, as the advertisements proclaim, double the space in your motorcaravan with an annexe tent. Most of those sold to motorcaravanners are the drive-away type. In plain English, that means a separate tent with some sort of sleeve for attachment to the vehicle, so that it is possible to walk from one to the other without going outside. A few motorcaravan dealers specialise in annexes and, although you may be nearer a tent-camping shop, the former will have expert knowledge about the difficulties of attaching the thing to the vehicle.

Whether you favour an annexe, or go for the biggest motorcaravan you can put up with, will depend upon your lifestyle. As an annexe is essentially a tent, it will take half an hour or so to put up, with poles and canvas to sort out and thirty or more pegs to bang into the ground. That is no problem if you intend to stay on the campsite for a few days or more, but can be a confounded nuisance in wet weather or if you are constantly on the move. However, an annexe tent is well worth the inconvenience if there are children. They will enjoy having their own playroom, might even like to sleep in it, thus relieving the congestion in the caravan. A corner can be curtained off to provide a toilet/dressing room, if you are of an independent nature or resent the trudge to the toilet block.

There is a compromise between a full annexe and nothing—an awning. This will slide into a channel screwed permanently to the side of the vehicle and be supported by just two or three poles, guy lines and pegs. It will take only a few minutes to put up, but must be taken down before driving away. An awning will provide top and, possibly, side cover, and is useful when the weather is warm and wet or hot and dry. Even less trouble, and ready in seconds, is the roller-blind awning imported from America. It works rather

As the advertisements proclaim, an annexe will double the size of a small motorcaravan

like a shop blind and can be entirely supported by the vehicle (and therefore used on hard standing) or with legs pegged to the ground. Guy ropes are necessary only in very windy conditions. Side and end curtains are available which will make it into a full annexe but of course they take time to assemble. There is always a price on convenience. An 'instant' roller-blind awning will cost as much or more than a full free-standing tent annexe.

Sanitation
The question of sanitation means a lot to some people. Others ignore it, relying on whatever is provided along the roads or at a campsite. Without doubt, there is going to come a time when you wish there was a lavatory in or beside the vehicle. It could be because of sickness or upset tummies, because the weather is foul or the site's facilities repugnant. There are two things my wife and I prefer about larger motorcaravans: the extra space and the walk-in, always available loo.

The various types of chemical closets will be covered in Chapter 11. Here we are concerned with use and management. Even the smallest van can carry one, perhaps tucked away in a locker or on full view, disguised with a cover as a seat. On site, it will be placed in a toilet tent or corner of the annexe. There are many possible solutions and I think I have tried most of them. There was the Volkswagen, where a canvas curtain was suspended from the open tailgate and pegged to the ground at just four points. A plywood shutter sealed the hole left at the rear by raising the tailgate. For use on roads in France (where, unlike their motorways, loos are a problem) we hung a curtain in the form of a small toilet tent inside the caravan—so much quicker and less conspicuous than pulling curtains over all the windows. On another van, a folding clothes airer was clipped to the side with canvas hung from that and pegged to the ground. These adaptations were designed to be in use more quickly than the average, free-standing toilet tent.

Emptying the chemical closet becomes less of a problem each year, as more and more sites, at home and abroad, provide the proper facilities. There was a time, ten years or more ago, when the British contingent could be spotted, at dead of night, creeping furtively to the site's lavatories, ashamed of their emptying chores. Nowadays, the CC disposal point is becoming the men's gossip centre. In Britain, Caravan Club sites have always led the way in this respect, providing proper disposal facilities for both grey and black water (washing-up and sewage). Only in the remotest areas, or perhaps when camping on a farm, is it necessary to take a spade, remove turf and dig your own hole—not forgetting to replace the turf. The fully equipped motorcaravan will still carry a spade 'just in case'. It might get you out of a snowdrift, or be useful on the beach.

That, when all is said and done, is what motorcaravanning is all about: being equipped at all times to take advantage of every opportunity or cope with any contingency.

8
Campsites—and non-sites

There are thousands of campsites crowded into the British Isles, though it is often difficult to find a single one when it is most needed. Signs are occasionally apparent on main roads but, in the nature of things, will never be obvious when you are looking for one. The official sign, approved by the Department of Transport, is the only one that may legally be exhibited as a road sign. It consists of an outline picture of an easily recognisable tent or caravan, an arrow indicating the direction to be taken and an indication of the distance.

These signs immediately place motorcaravanners in a quandary, for there is no indication whether, under our peculiar licensing system, such vehicles will be accepted. Generally, there is no need to worry. In practically every case, if trailer caravans may park there, so can motorcaravans. The few exceptions would be due to the personal whim of the owner of the site—the same sort of prejudice that many car drivers on crowded roads feel for trailer caravanners.

Occasionally motorcaravans will be banned from a site because the owner genuinely thinks it is unsuitable, most likely because all the ground is sloping. He knows that trailer caravans are fitted with legs at each corner which allow the outfit to cope with sloping ground. He does not know that the well-equipped motorcaravanner carries ramps or boards which enable him, too, to stand level on sloping or uneven ground. Admittedly though, it is more troublesome to level a motorcaravan and we would all choose a level pitch for preference. However, in the vast majority of cases, sites that take caravans will welcome motorcaravanners. Tents-only sites are a bit more of a puzzle.

At one time, tents could be pitched almost anywhere and required no planning permission. Farmers in popular holiday areas found it more profitable to harvest tents than crops. Shades of those easier days linger on and there are still some local authorities who look upon tents as less evil, less damaging to the landscape than caravans. As a matter of simple fact, the reverse is true. You have only got to inspect a pitch recently vacated by a modern frame tent to realise this. The grass, or what is left of it, will be yellow and exude a rotten smell, for it has not been able to breathe through the waterproof groundsheet. It will take weeks to recover and may never do so if another and yet another tent is allowed to pitch on the same spot. The caravan, on the other hand, will leave six tiny yellow squares, two resulting from the wheels and four from the packing pieces beneath the corner steadies — perhaps one more from the jockey wheel if that has been left down. The motorcaravan is likely to leave no trace, for the chances are that it will be driven on an excursion during the daytime and the few blades of grass that have been flattened by the wheels will soon spring back to life. It is just possible you may need to quote this argument to an uncooperative site manager at some time. Even if caravanners and motorcaravanners use annexes, there is not always going to be dead grass to betray where they have been, for several of them do not use groundsheets.

Caravans and motorcaravans cause little if any damage to the environment — they are here today, gone tomorrow, or soon after. The difficulty is that some people confuse touring caravans with the eyesores that have for years ruined much of Britain's coastline: static holiday caravans. These are let out by the week and are a highly profitable investment for landowners. I have not forgotten that they make it possible for some families to have a holiday which they could afford in no other way. But if only they could be called 'chalets' rather than 'caravans' — and their owners would spread them out more and take an interest in land-scaping. For ideas, they should visit some of the best touring sites.

Back to sites for tents. Some, strangely, will accept motorcaravans, others will not. Sometimes it is the likes or dislikes of the site owner that decides, in other cases it is the peculiar requirements of planning permission. To be fair, it could also be the suitability of the roads leading to the site. Narrow roads that can cope with cars and average motorcaravans might be entirely unsuitable for cars towing caravans, for there is always going to be the occasion when two such outfits meet head on and there is no passing space. A motorcaravan is not the easiest vehicle to reverse in a narrow lane (until the driver has learnt to use his door mirrors, anyway) but a trailer combination is virtually impossible in such circumstances. So, the only way to discover whether a site for tents will accept motorcaravans is to ask.

Better still, invest in a book of sites. There are many on sale and there will be a fair selection in most large bookshops and railway station bookstalls. Be discriminating in your choice. Try, especially, to distinguish between those which recommend sites because they have been inspected and those which are obviously influenced by advertisement revenue.

The books published by the motoring organisations are on general sale and not restricted to members, though the latter may be able to buy at favourable prices. They are very good and wholly trustworthy within their terms of reference. Do remember, though, that the number of stars or pennants does not necessarily refer to the quality of the site or the warmth of welcome you are likely to receive. It is primarily a record of the number (not the quality) of 'amenities' — in exactly the same way as a hotel with a bath to every bedroom will be rated higher than one with shared bathrooms.

I like enormously the highly subjective books published by Alan Rogers. He visits every site listed, whether in Britain or on the Continent, and writes half a page or so about it. He admits, honestly, if a particular site is included (in spite of a few complaints from users of previous years' guides) because it is the only one in the area, is conveniently near to a through route, or for some other compelling reason. One may not always agree with him, but he has never let us down significantly and his descriptions make enjoyable reading.

The fullest descriptions of sites at home and abroad are to be found in the camping and caravanning monthly magazines. These are often sent in by readers, hoping for and no doubt receiving some small payment. As a result, they are highly subjective impressions and, examining the 'letters' pages, you will often find that a place praised one month is vehemently criticised later. It is not always the fault of the original contributor. A site that is delightful in, say, June, can look fairly tatty towards the tail end of August, when grass and staff are tired and the toilet rooms have suffered from their share of vandals. If you take a monthly magazine it may be worth cutting out and filing the site reports listed therein, or, if you treasure the books, making notes. However, the selection is too random and haphazard to be of more than coincidental use.

There is one very hopeful development on the British sites scene called 'Best of British'. It is a loose association (their wording) of a dozen or so top-class campsites spread over the mainland, begun in the hope that it will spread to about a score, or not much more. They are all privately owned and run or closely supervised by their proprietors, who elect a committee to inspect one another's campgrounds. They insist upon the very highest standards, run spot checks on one another and will suspend anyone who fails to keep his site up to standard. This is no idle boast. There has already been one suspension. It is a highly laudable scheme and deserves to receive support from the public.

Oddly enough, a site guide is not nearly so necessary abroad (especially in France) as in Britain. Every town seems to have its 'camping' sign in the form of a tent, for the city fathers and parish councillors have long recognised the value of tourism to the local community. On the Continent, this sign means that nearby there is a place catering not only for tents, but caravans, motorcaravans, trailer tents, pup tents, cycle campers and even the hardy folk who snuggle down beneath the stars in waterproof sleeping bags. Some well-ordered sites do separate the little tents from the big caravans. As in Britain, several sites have residential or holiday caravans; in France, there is sometimes a permanent population of 'gipsies' but the *gardien* is likely to direct tourists to the quietest spot.

Abroad, though, as at home, you are more likely to find the best camping sites if you plan ahead and, again, this means books. Yet again, there are several, but the best known and most easily available in this country is *Michelin Camping & Caravanning France*. It is printed in French, with introductions in other languages (including English). An hour's study will enable anyone with no French whatsoever to understand and use it to advantage. The problem with *Michelin* and many other similar guides, at home or abroad, is the number of confusing symbols that must be learnt and remembered. Very few publishers now offer a bookmark on which the symbols are printed so, if your memory is as bad as mine, you waste precious time thumbing back to the key, probably losing your place in the meantime. That is a minor annoyance if you are planning your next port of call in a leisurely way the night before; it is a real aggravation if you have stopped illegally on a busy road and are being blasted by powerful horns. (There is never a layby when it is most needed!)

My favourite site guides come from the Caravan Club. The

book for Britain and Ireland cannot be bought. It is issued free to members once every two years, with a supplement updating it in the intervening years and news of any other changes printed in the magazine sent to members at more or less regular intervals. Within its covers are listed about 150 Club Sites, thousands of 'certificated locations' and a sprinkling of licensed sites open to the general public. Certificated locations are small, informal sites available only to members, and usually attached to farms, though some may be in a field behind a pub and others, specifically termed 'night halts', attached to filling stations. 'CLs', as members call them, are restricted to five outfits by law, so there will not be any glamorous toilet blocks or bingo parlours. More than likely there will just be a tap from which to draw water and a hole for the contents of the chemical closet. But farmers' wives have been known to sell really fresh eggs and other farm produce and one or two have even gone so far as to offer take-away home cooking. Other clubs list certificated locations for their members, but I do not know of any with the tremendous selection offered by the Caravan Club.

The Caravan Club's overseas book is on sale to members. It is worth belonging just for that, being a glowing example of the sort of unpaid cooperation that is a prominent feature of most such clubs. The 700-plus page book is packed with reports from members, telling you how to find the sites (in English, of course) and what to expect when you get there. It is easy to understand, because there is a complete absence of symbols and the few abbreviations are soon mastered. The Club's knowledgeable officials have added notes about motoring in each country, plus a lot more essential information. As only about 5 per cent of the Caravan Club's quarter of a million members are motorcaravanners, information is angled towards motorists towing caravans. So there are a few passages that can be skipped, but 99 per cent is relevant. All the other clubs listed in Appendix 3 (see page 186) offer lists of sites in Britain and abroad. The Caravan Club, because it is the largest, has the most to offer, but some motorcaravanners may prefer the specialised, more personal approach of the smaller organisations.

The motoring organisations and clubs all supply full information and plenty of advice about camping and motoring abroad. No one, presumably, would be foolish enough to leave his home base without some sort of insurance (for vehicle and occupants), guarantee of recovery (again, vehicle and occupants) and documentation, so this will not be discussed here. My purpose throughout this book is to supply information which is difficult to get by other means, and to tell readers where to look up what they do not know. So I wholeheartedly recommend membership of one of the clubs for the information and back-up that they offer.

Many join a club for another reason—the social aspect. Clubs are permitted to run 'rallies' on land that is not licensed for camping and the weekend get-together is the highlight of many motorcaravanners' lives. All sorts of activities take place, including coffee mornings, when members gather for a chat and perhaps a raffle. None of the clubs subsidise these social activities out of general funds (rather the reverse) so there is no question of any part of your subscription enabling other people to have a jolly good time. Weekend (and longer holiday) rallies do, however, provide a guaranteed pitch for those who book in advance and there is often room for the ones who just turn up. A considerable amount of thought is given to the venues, which are often chosen because there is something interesting to see or do nearby. It might be just a beach or beautiful part of the country, or there may be something happening, like a traction-engine rally or medieval jousting. The possibilities are endless and offer an alternative to just going to a campsite for a weekend and hoping for the best.

Overseas rallies are a different matter from those at home. Some will be based on one campsite for the whole duration, others will have you moving to another site every few days. It is not usual to drive in convoy (almost impossible on today's roads) though a couple of families may agree to keep each other in sight. There is the chance to chat with others who speak the same language. Coach tours to places of interest nearby will give the drivers a rest from having to cope with strange roads and stranger traffic behaviour. Sometimes there is a civic reception or an invitation to visit wine caves. Always there is someone to help with any problems that may occur.

There is another, rather more expensive way of easing some of the difficulties of foreign travel and site finding that is especially recommended to apprehensive first timers abroad. (After the first time, you will know how easy it all is.) Canvas Holidays were the first to offer ready erected tents at campsites in France. The idea has spread to most of Europe and many other firms have joined the pioneers. It may seem nonsense to drive a perfectly respectable motorcaravan hundreds of miles so that you can go and live in a tent. But think on. All documentation, insurance and ferry booking is arranged for you and included in the price. You are guaranteed a pitch on a first class campsite — in the high season if you wish (and that is something you would have difficulty in finding yourself). There are English speaking couriers to act as your hosts, put you wise to what is on and what to avoid locally, and to deal with any problems. The spacious and fully equipped tents will come almost as an unlooked-for bonus but they will be especially appreciated by motorcaravanners with large families in small vehicles.

We Hunts, although not first timers, have used the system simply because we wanted to be guaranteed a good pitch in a popular area. We have found that Eurocamp work to the same high standards as Canvas Holidays. I suppose we reached the height of absurdity when we booked a six-berth static caravan through Freshfields on a site in Brittany and drove there in our spacious motorhome. It *was* expensive, especially for two people, but we lived in luxury and still spent less than we would have done in an hotel.

It is a sad fact of life that nowadays it is necessary to book a pitch at campsites in popular areas during the high season — sad, because it is the very negation of the 'free-to-roam' image popularised by the makers of motorcaravans. If you want a site near the sea in Britain or abroad during July and August, you must book well ahead, not days, but weeks and sometimes months. Arriving 'on spec' you will need to motor a few miles inland, and this applies to the south of France as well as the south of England.

Some motorcaravanners get around the problem by 'wild camping'. Perhaps, in this instance, 'free camping' would be a more accurate description. They can be seen parked on promenades in towns as far apart as Blackpool and Nice, where they hope to get away with it for a night or two, often to the annoyance of local residents and hoteliers, who badger their authorities to get something done about it. Such free campers, unwittingly or unheedingly, harm the public image of motorcaravanning. One must sympathise with the family who, having driven for hours, find there is just nowhere to park. Tired and hungry, they are probably safer offending the residents than in continuing to drive. One hopes that, refreshed, they will move on to another place. Some just take root, and it is that which causes offence, or real animosity if there are several doing the same thing.

Nearly all experienced motorcaravanners will have camped wild at some time or another, whether perforce or from choice. There is no harm in doing so, provided certain guidelines are observed. First and foremost, it is essential to avoid giving offence to anyone. So do not camp in a residential area, because some resident is not going to like it. If there is a solitary house somewhere out in the wilds, make yourself known. If, in spite of your best endeavours, opposition is expressed, move on. Wherever you end up, do not take root, or give the impression of doing so. If it is absolutely essential to remove items from the caravan before you can use the beds, avoid scattering them around; instead, make a neat pile on the side of the vehicle that is most likely to be away from public view. Wild campers should, however, plan matters so that there is no need to put anything outside. Lines of washing strung between trees or smalls draped over bushes are particularly unsightly. Buy or make a clothes drying horse that hangs on the side of the vehicle or clips over a window channel or gutter.

Numbers of wild campers are a give-away and very likely to arouse opposition. 'Two's company, three's a crowd' should be your maxim. When overnighting in some solitary spot, the presence of another vehicle is comforting and could, in fact, offer real security against vandals, muggers or bandits. Lone motorcaravanners have suffered from the attentions of the latter, in some of the Mediterranean countries. In some countries abroad, where there are no campsites, motorcaravanners are allowed to gather in greater numbers. If they congregate on or near a remote beach on, for instance, one of the Canary Islands, nobody is going to bother them. If they set up house in numbers on the promenade of the only town, it is unlikely that they will be left in peace for long.

With the increasing popularity of motorcaravanning in all European countries, the opportunities for wild camping are decreasing in direct proportion. So those who at present claim that they never spend a penny on site fees had better start saving. The days of free camping in most civilised countries are numbered. Make the most of it while you can.

There are places where it is most inadvisable to park overnight and prominent among them are car parks in or on the outskirts of big cities, especially in the Mediterranean countries. Police supervision is not all it might be, and several alarming stories of attacks on vehicles and occupants have reached me. In general, you seem to be safer the further north you go, but many a motorcaravan can be seen overnighting in town squares (not big cities) in France. Foreigners (that means you—not the French) should ask permission at the local *gendarmerie* or *mairie*, for they are supposed to register somewhere overnight. You cannot 'register', however, overnighting in the rest area on a French autoroute. It is a suitable place for a couple of outfits to stop (one might feel lonely and vulnerable) and is a practice that is tolerated at time of writing. Loners would be well advised to use the lorry parks at the service areas, alongside many drivers snatching a nap in their cabs. The bustle of the morning departure of the enormous commercials will ensure an early awakening and prompt start for motorcaravanners, too.

In some countries, you have a right to free camp for one night, in others it is strictly forbidden—to an extent that passports could be impounded. The clubs' and motoring associations' overseas-camping handbooks will contain up-to-date information.

In Britain, the official line is that it is up to the owner of the land, and all land belongs to someone. You may sleep in your motorcaravan in the driveway of a friend's house (unless there happens to be a bye-law or clause in his deeds forbidding it), in a pub's car park, a farmer's field or wherever you can think of, with the permission of the owner. There is a time limit, but we are talking about overnighting. You are unlikely to get permission to stay in a town's car park, on common land or in a layby. Laybys are a special case, being provided for resting. Who can say when a 'rest' becomes a 'camp'? Often you will be untroubled overnight, sometimes a policeman will knock on the door to ensure that you are not in trouble, or to move you on. Note that sidelights should be switched on in laybys, unless there is a notice to the contrary. And if you are asked to move on, do so without argument, for you have no rights in this instance.

All in all, it is easier to use proper campsites and how you should behave on them is all commonsense, a matter of not causing annoyance to your neighbours and leaving the pitch bearing no signs of your occupancy. But I would recommend, in any country, that you have a nose around before booking in. Many parents send children running off to look at the lavatories. If they return pinching their noses, the message is obvious and you will move on unless desperate for a rest.

Campers can choose their sites but what is not always appreciated is that sites have an equal right to choose their campers. Some are very particular, refusing entry to solo motorcyclists, groups of teenagers, backpackers, and big motorhomes. The latter restriction applies particularly to converted buses and coaches but I once received some suspicious glances when I drove on to a Caravan Club site in an enormous American motorhome which was being road tested. Production of the membership card smoothed the way but the warden did make some ploy about siting the rig where it would not affect the susceptibilities of respectable trailer caravanners.

I would like to round off this chapter with a debating point. On many sites, a couple in a tiny, crawl-in tent will be charged less than a caravanner with a large motorhome. Children usually qualify for half price and even OAPs sometimes expect a reduction. Seems fair? Think a bit.

A site is not run by the social services department for the benefit of the underprivileged. It is there to make a profit and, just as parents with large families expect to come out of a supermarket with a larger bill than, say, a childless couple, so should campsite users pay for the amenities they need to take advantage of. The couple in the pup tent will want somewhere to wash clothes, vegetables and themselves. In foul weather they will expect a recreation room and entertainment in the form of a television. They will rely on lavatories being provided and kept clean. In short, they will need everything the site has to offer. The owner of the big motorhome, who needs nothing more than a water supply and disposal point, demands far less of the site and is expected to subsidise the less adequately equipped. 'He can afford to', you may say. But should he have to?

9
Keeping out of trouble

There was a small swelling above my right eye, probably a developing spot or a boil. It might turn out to be a minor nuisance but was certainly no reason for cancelling the holiday. So, on the day before we were due to sail from Southampton on the morning boat, we motored down to the Solent Motel. In the morning my face had swollen to such an extent that the eyes had become slits. Yet I felt nothing and ate a reasonable breakfast. There was no necessity for explanations to the staff when I asked the way to the nearest doctor. A nearby group practice was recommended and we made our way there with all speed.

'All the doctors have full appointment books,' said the receptionist. 'Can you come back tomorrow?' I explained carefully and politely that the boat sailed in a couple of hours and that it was unlikely that the captain could be persuaded to wait that long. This was Southampton and the mention of boat and sailing produced immediate results.

In no time at all I was given a consultation, injection and a prescription. We were away in a flash, parked on a double yellow line to collect the pills from the chemist, and made a dash for the boat, arriving first in the queue, with an hour or more to spare. I never did discover exactly what had been wrong with me but am relieved to be able to report that I was back to normal shape in the promised couple of days, thanking Aneurin Bevan, Lord Beveridge and the British taxpayer for our good old health service.

Insurance
This tale is told because it has a moral: BE INSURED. In Britain, you have no option. Across the water, things are different. There is no shortage of medical treatment available, provided you can pay for it on the spot or can produce proof that it will be paid for. That is where a good insurance back-up is invaluable. One phone call is all it takes, to a London number that is manned twenty-four hours a day, and it is nearly always direct dialling nowadays.

In France, for instance, if you have the francs in your pocket, you pay in advance in cash. Then, if that leaves you short or the injury or illness involves hospital treatment, your London contact will take over responsibility. All you do is sit back and be treated. If you are really ill, you may be flown home in an air ambulance and a driver will be provided to recover the motorcaravan if there is no other driver in your party.

Insurance policies vary, of course. I have quoted an example of the best, assuming you have not tried to economise by trimming off benefits. When abroad you can, if you so wish or think it wise, rely solely on the reciprocal health agreements applicable in the various countries. As an example, in France, you pay for treatment and medicines, collecting little stamps as you do so, which have then to be converted back into francs. All very well if you speak French, understand a system which is more bureaucratic than ours, and have the stamina to see it through. The exercise is begun, long before the holiday begins, by filling in Form E111, which is obtainable from the local office of the Department of Health and Social Security. In fact, Form E111 often arrives through the post with your travel and insurance documents. You are advised to fill it in and send it off, anyway, for the DHSS will then send you another form which provides proof of your entitlement to medical or hospital treatment. With your own insurance too, it is a sort of belt and braces policy.

It is the same for the vehicle. You are not now asked to produce a 'Green Card' at frontiers, for the UK car insurance covers you — but only to a limited extent. The fact that it may be comprehensive at home has no bearing, unless you have taken out a Green Card, which extends the provisions of your policy to all the countries named thereon. Travelling without one could land you with a hefty bill which would have to be paid from your own resources.

The vehicle insurers will ask, when you apply for the Green Card, if you intend travelling in Spain. A 'bail bond' is highly desirable there, if you want to be sure of staying out of prison. If you should happen to be involved in a road accident, you are likely to be held in custody until responsibilities for the mishap have been sorted out and until you can prove your ability to pay any damages that may be awarded against you. The bail bond provides such proof and it would indeed be a foolhardy motorcaravanner who ignored it for the sake of saving a pound or two on holiday expenses. Some vehicle insurers, by the way, now offer free Green Cards for a limited period. Free bail bonds may be the next inducement.

Having insured yourself, everyone travelling with you, and the vehicle, it might also be advisable to take out cancellation cover, so that you can recover at least part of the money you will have paid out in advance. It is worth, at least, studying the small print on the booking forms to ascertain the position should illness or calamity force abandonment of the holiday.

There is one more item of insurance that motorcaravanners must take out and it costs only a few pence. Any camper who has been abroad will know that the camping carnet is essential unless, perhaps, you are going for a fully booked package deal. A carnet can be obtained from a club or motoring organisation and most people treat it as an identity card for campsite use. Unless you pay site fees in advance (a procedure that is advisable if the stay is for one night only) the carnet, which bears your photograph, will be retained at the site office until you settle the bill and leave. If you have no carnet, your passport will probably be demanded— particularly in Switzerland. That is fair enough, but I will not surrender mine in such circumstances and, if the demand continues, will offer full payment in advance. If that does not work, the only alternative is to go elsewhere. Do not ever surrender a passport, except to a uniformed police officer. Even then, it is advisable to demand a receipt.

The carnet, in addition to being an identity card, gives the site owner some sort of assurance that, if you abscond, the issuing organisation will at least consider making good his losses. More important to him is the little stamp it bears, assuring him that the bearer is covered by third party insurance. If you should accidentally damage another camper or a building on the site, there is insurance cover, provided the little stamp is up to date (it must be renewed yearly). This cover does not extend to any damage caused by a motor vehicle. That will carry its own third party insurance. If it does not, or the policy has lapsed, you could be in deep trouble. If you are away for a long time and have not been able to renew the policy (arrangements should really be made with your insurers before you leave) third party cover can be obtained at customs posts, or they will tell you where to go to get it. If you do not speak the language, produce the insurance certificate and point to the expiry date. That, accompanied by a little mime, should do the trick. Do not, on any account, drive around uninsured hoping for the best.

Documents and money

With all these documents, and a lot more, you will need somewhere safe to keep them. A plastic document wallet is ideal and can be found in most stationery shops. Inside, there are several tough plastic envelopes, which can be labelled in permanent pen with their contents.

I have referred to my own wallet as a check that nothing is omitted from the 'essential' list which follows. These are the contents of the envelopes:

1 *Tickets and passport*   Ferry tickets are the first documents that are going to be needed, followed immediately afterwards by the passport which, once you are on board the ferry, should be removed and treasured in pocket or handbag as carefully as a wallet and cheque book.

2 *Vehicle registration and Green Card*   In addition to the Green Card, which extends the vehicle's insurance policy to named countries, it is necessary to take the registration document, which is valuable and must not be lost. I have been asked to produce it twice in twenty years: once in a spot check by French traffic police (who did not notice that the colour of the vehicle was incorrect—I had been busy with a paint brush) and once by customs officials on our return to Britain, who could not understand why I was driving a left-hand drive Volkswagen if I was not trying to import it illegally. It was a 'special' on loan for road test.

3 *Camping*   This envelope will hold the camping carnet and the sites directory which contains details of and instructions for reaching the first night's campsite. If we were going to a booked site, the necessary documents would also be enclosed.

4 *Maps*   My road map (usually a *Michelin* in France) will be readily available on top of the dashboard in the cab. Other maps which might be useful are in the envelope. They include the small scale, large area maps which are given away by tourist offices in London, perhaps some town plans, and anything else which is not too bulky and directly relevant to the holiday. More maps, accumulated over the years, which might just conceivably be of some use, are relegated to a carrier bag under

one of the seats, together with guidebooks and the mass of literature which comes through the post when you write to a tourist office.

5 *Breakdown, medical, accident*   This envelope gets fairly bulky and has to be thinned down at regular intervals. Essential components are the vehicle insurance policy, bearing the reference number which must be quoted if you should have to telephone for assistance or a spare part, and, of course, the emergency telephone number. A list of dialling codes from foreign countries saves the aggravation of trying to find the vital number in an unfamiliar telephone directory, even if a directory can be found. There is also a dictionary of the names of car parts and common emergency phrases (such as 'my brakes don't work') picked up in an AA bookshop.

Then there is the vital 'Certificate of Entitlement to Benefits in Kind during a Stay in a Member State' which comes free from the DHSS once you have sent off Form E111, plus the information 'How to get Medical Treatment in other EEC Countries' and 'Medical Treatment during Visits Abroad' which proclaims: 'Medical treatment is extremely expensive . . . you are strongly recommended to follow the advice about private insurance.' And that is official. So our private medical insurance documents are also here, together with a note of our National Insurance numbers because we can never remember them when asked.

My motor insurance company also supplied a leaflet with instructions about the overseas claims service. It gives names, addresses and telephone numbers of their representatives (claims adjusters) in all countries likely to be visited. The bit about Spain bears repetition: 'If you are involved in a motor accident, however trivial, it is essential you contact our representative . . . the Green Card offers no guarantee against detention . . . our representative is able to take immediate steps to obtain the release from detention of the Insured . . .' The bail bond is a vital document for travellers to Spain.

Lastly, there is the European Accident Statement, issued with the Green Card by the motor insurance company. This will be dealt with later in this chapter.

6 *Miscellaneous*   This last envelope is the escape route for muddled thinkers like me. It is planned to take anything that

does not seem to have a home anywhere else and is inclined to accumulate receipts from restaurants, admission tickets to ancient monuments and the like, with scribbled comments so that we can tell our friends about places to visit and to avoid. At the moment, it contains about half a dozen surplus 'GB' stickers. Ever since ours fell off and I had to do a quick DIY job with a felt pen, I have carried a spare and have, on occasion, helped out a fellow compatriot in trouble. I suppose these GB stickers, which arrive unasked with ferry tickets and insurance packages, should have some value abroad, for they are unobtainable on the other side of the channel.

The envelopes in their folder form a package which can be kept in the cab, immediately available when needed. When leaving the vehicle unattended, we take only the vital, irreplaceable ones with us, along with handbag or camera gadget box which, between them, hold cheque books, cheque and credit cards and personal paraphernalia. It is unfortunate, but there always seems to be something to carry around.

Spread your money and travellers' cheques around so that, if pick-pocketed, at least something will be left. Cheque books, cheque cards and credit cards should never all be in the same pocket or handbag compartment, yet must be readily available when needed. Credit cards are becoming increasingly useful and, to save carrying a lot of cash, we look out for fuel stations with the 'Visa' sign. Do ensure, however that the chit is examined carefully before it is signed. I know one motorcaravanner who was billed for 700 francs instead of 70 because an extra 'O' had crept in. Barclaycard queried the bill for him with the owner of the garage concerned but he got nowhere. The garage man's tale that he had bought some accessories was believed. It helps if a bill is itemised. There are not many motorcaravans that could take on board what would have amounted to about £70 worth of petrol.

Since 1983, UK cheques and cheque cards are useless abroad. You need special Eurocheques from your bank. Travellers' cheques are so well known that no comment is necessary here. Just remember to observe the instructions.

First aid

A first-aid kit is a legal requirement in many countries and one motorcaravanner in Yugoslavia described how the police had demanded to see his stock of bandages. They then proceeded to measure them to ensure that they conformed to the stipulated recommendation. Our friend, not easily frightened, then asked to see theirs. They were duly produced, and found to be filthy. In normal circumstances, a well-filled first-aid box should satisfy investigators—but make sure that it contains a plentiful supply of bandages and slings as well as eye and injury pads. The type that is packed in a cushion is preferable because it does not become a dangerous projectile in a sudden stop. The obligatory first-aid kit should be in addition to plasters and personal medicaments and remedies, some of which will be needed in the normal course of events. Common remedies should be available in the shops, but there is the hassle of finding the right shop when needed and identifying the brand with the right ingredients. It is easier to take your favourite aspirins, indigestion remedies, tummy settlers and all the other essentials of civilised living.

Do not forget the Dettol, or whatever antiseptic you use. I once cut my foot quite badly in the sea in France, but the motorcaravan was nearby and a good soaking in a bowl of diluted Dettol, plus a cup of tea, soon put me right. A tight bandage and frequent cleaning for a couple of days ensured that there was no further trouble. Another time, my wife caught her foot in a hole in the ground, twisted her ankle as she fell and was near to passing out with nausea. A quick sniff of smelling salts enabled her to limp back to our mobile home, for hot and cold compresses.

When motoring abroad do your best to observe speed limits. The days when the ignorant foreigner could get away with a spot of law breaking because he did not know any better have long gone. Admittedly, the chance of being 'done' for failure to observe a speed limit is 100 to 1 against in nearly all European countries, it seems. As to whether you are willing to run the remote risk of an on-the-spot fine is one for you to decide. Just do not blindly imitate everyone else, for you could be the unlucky one to get caught. The overseas handbooks of clubs and motoring organisations will tell you exactly what current speed restrictions are on motorways and other places where they may not be marked. The name board at the approach to a French town, for instance, marks the beginning of the urban speed limit. There is enough about motoring abroad to fill the rest of this book, so do invest in a handbook.

Breakdowns

If your motorcaravan breaks down on the road, be consoled by the thought that it could not happen in a more suitable vehicle, and do not panic. Take the necessary safety precautions first. Switch on the hazard flashers and walk back to place the safety triangle in the road, out a little way from the gutter or kerb so that it will be noticed by approaching motorists (on the hard shoulder on a motorway). The triangle, which you must carry, is essential for your safety if you have come to a halt just round a blind corner. If it happens to be on a fast road, too, start praying and, as an additional precaution, send a member of your party back to warn approaching traffic. (Arms held out, palms downwards with arms moved up and down seems to be generally understood as a 'slow down' signal; at night a torch should be waved if you do not possess a lantern with a flashing beacon.)

Provided the breakdown is in a place where you are not in imminent danger of being mown down by an approaching vehicle, it is probably best to remain on the road and cause some

A recovery service will get you home—but do make sure the one you choose can cope with a motorcaravan

sort of obstruction. Nobody is going to stop and thank you for exerting superhuman effort and pushing the vehicle on to the verge or a layby, where you will be no bother to anyone and likely to be ignored. If you inconvenience other traffic, somebody is going to do something about it in the way of offering help. This is where acting ability is an asset. You have got to make your plight understood by others. Make an exhibition of yourself. Get the children out if there are any but try to persuade them not to look too happy—difficult, because the chances are they will enjoy the experience. Lift the bonnet or engine cover, even if the trouble is elsewhere; it is a sign of distress.

Some motorcaravanners travelling abroad carry a small blackboard on which messages can be chalked. Look up, in the phrase book which has been supplied with your overseas touring package or insurance, the appropriate word for 'help' or 'breakdown' and hold it so that passing motorists can see it. Make a point of showing it to them and look them in the face. Ensure that the GB sticker is visible (it helps to have one on the front, too, and perhaps another on the blackboard). It would indeed be a hard-hearted Britisher who left a fellow countryman in the lurch.

All this applies on ordinary roads. Such an exhibition would be illegal on most motorways, when you must walk to the nearest telephone or wait for official assistance. When setting out for the telephone, do not forget to take full particulars of the vehicle with you, a phrase book, loose change, passport, and the British emergency telephone number if you are insured.

When help, or the promise of it, has arrived, take full advantage of the facilities of the motorcaravan. Brew tea or coffee (best to lay off alcohol at this stage) for the members of the party and offer a cup to whoever is giving assistance or effecting repairs. If it is to be a long wait, you will be glad your motorcaravan is fully equipped. This is one of the unexpected occasions when a chemical closet could prove invaluable. It is difficult to advise about abandoning the motorcaravan completely should this seem desirable. It might be stolen or vandalised. In some parts of southern Europe and northern Africa, in fairly isolated areas, the occupants could be at risk from robbers or bandits, in which case people are more important than the most treasured vehicle.

The European Accident Statement will be supplied with the Green Card by your motor insurers. It is a form to be filled in whenever you have an accident and is much better than the usual name, address and policy number scribbled on the back of an envelope because it reminds both you and the third party of all the information that later may be required to settle a claim. It does not constitute an admission of liability on the part of either driver, but should be signed by both, each retains one copy (there are two, self-duplicating). It would be just as useful for encounters of an unwanted kind in Britain. I do not know why it is issued only to motorists going abroad.

Do not be put off by the possibilities of breakdowns, accidents and hospitals. The chances are that you will have an enjoyable time and will later laugh about any small mishaps that may have come your way. My family still chide me about the time on our first holiday abroad when the petrol tank developed a leak and, after I had failed to cure it with chewing gum, Plasticine and soap (separately), we drove from garage to garage. At each one I knelt down beside the old motorcaravan, tried to mime the dripping and, for good measure, said 'plonk, plonk, plonk' hoping that would be understood in any language. The efficient Germans, Austrians and Swiss could not do anything. Succour eventually came in France. The tank was drained, removed, covered with mastic and replaced while we spent a day wandering around Nancy. The obliging receptionist at the Leyland agents would accept nothing for the work, but did allow me to give the mechanic a *pourboire*. Nowadays, the spares kit contains a bandage that is petrol proof, just in case.

Precautions

Though, according to the law of averages, a major calamity is unlikely to strike, there will inevitably be little inconveniences now and again. Getting lost at some time happens to all of us. The chances are that locals abroad will not understand your pronunciation of their town names. The blackboard already mentioned comes in here. Chalk the name of the next town and hold it up to pedestrians. They will catch on quickly and point the way, may even, if offered the chalk, draw a little map. If you are seeking a campsite, draw the international symbol of a little tent and a question mark. The blackboard, or a note pad, comes into its own, too, when you cannot find what you need in shop or supermarket.

At a continental filling station, I pulled up beside a petrol pump and indicated to the attendant that the tank was to be filled. He waved me forward a few feet, then started to fill the tank. Fortunately, I had dismounted from the driving seat and saw that the diesel pump was being used. My panic cry of 'STOP!' was understood before any damage was done. (A pint or so of diesel oil in 12 gallons of petrol had no apparent effect on performance.) I do not know why it was assumed that diesel was required. The youngster probably thought all vans used it. The moral is obvious: get out and supervise, and make sure that the pump is set to zero before delivery commences, unless you are willing to pay for petrol you have not had.

Do not assume that a vehicle which runs well on two star at home will be happy on the lowest grade abroad. You will not do any damage by having petrol of a higher octane rating than needed, but lower it too much and valves could suffer. If you are filling an almost empty tank, go first for 'super'; use some and then top up with low grade. Use a bit more, and top up again. At the first sign of 'pinking' or loss of performance, revert to super and adjust future fillings so that the proportion of low-grade petrol is not increased.

You should not, of course, motor with any gas appliance burning, although it is not illegal to do so in Britain under certain circumstances. It is definitely illegal—and foolhardy—to enter any filling station (or ferry or tunnel) with even a pilot light aglow. If you are chancing your luck, remember to stop and turn off the gas before reaching the pumps. As can be detected from its smell, petrol vapour travels through the air and can be ignited by any naked flame. It has happened, more than once. Trailer and motorcaravans with refrigerators operating on gas have become balls of fire when taking on petrol.

Sensible precautions must be taken when camping. Make sure the motorcaravan is level, using levelling ramps if necessary. It is not only more comfortable that way but safer, because pans will not tend to slide off gas rings. A gas refrigerator will not work for more than about half an hour if it is more than a few degrees off dead level, even if it is being run on mains electricity. An airlock will form which can sometimes be dispersed by driving on rough roads. More often the refrigerator must be removed and inverted.

If there is a chance to couple a properly equipped motorcaravan to mains electricity, observe polarity, ensure that plugs are pushed right home and that connecting leads do not trail where others could trip over them. In damp conditions especially, switch off at source before making or breaking connections and, preferably, wear rubber boots and gloves.

In hot countries it can be tempting to park beneath trees. Please yourself, but take account of the possibility of sticky secretions spoiling the coachwork and of the annoying drip, drip, drip on to the roof in wet weather. Trees with dead branches should be avoided.

If the ground looks soggy, think about departure next day. It is better to be at the top of a slope than in a hollow. Keep driven wheels as near as possible to a hard road or track; choose a hard standing if there is one.

As soon as you are settled, send out a reconnaissance party to discover the facilities, times of opening of any shop, location of fire extinguishers and what to do in an emergency. Find out where the site warden lives or a telephone is sited in case somebody is taken ill suddenly.

In the motorcaravan itself, there should always be some form of ventilation, more so when the cooker or a gas heater is in use. Condensation can be a real problem at any time but it is always aggravated by insufficient ventilation. Try, however, to arrange open windows so that an intruder or sneak thief cannot take advantage of them when all occupants are asleep. I know one motorcaravanner who hung his trousers near a partly opened window. They were gone in the morning but more serious was the loss of his wallet. On the whole, fellow campers are honest. Thieving is more likely on large, crowded sites in popular tourist areas. Hide handbags, cameras and all valuables at all times.

For peace of mind, spare a thought for the vehicle each day. You may have motored far and fast, especially if abroad. In addition to the usual camping chores, adopt a routine for daily inspection of oil and water levels, occasional but regular checks on battery and tyre pressures. Lie down and take a look underneath sometimes, not forgetting to examine the hidden sides of the tyre walls. With a little forethought and an easy routine of maintenance and checks, you should enjoy all your motorcaravanning, at home and abroad.

10
Motorcaravanning as a way of life — Mary Tisdall

Nowadays a motorcaravan is likely to be the first experience some have of the open road. How fortunate they are to experience the joys of this self-contained method of travel. Motorised caravans enable people to have an independence and freedom of movement that gives a new outlook to their lives. Suitable for all age groups, there is no class barrier: be they vintage, home conversions or newly bought motorcaravans, all will happily mingle with one another.

My husband Archie and I had used tents and caravans before we bought our first motorcaravan, so we had some experience of camping. This is not essential in any way: many first-time owners take successfully to their new way of life without any previous experience of outdoor travelling. Over the years we have met a wonderfully varied number of happy motorcaravanners and only very occasionally have we encountered someone who has not taken to the new environment. It could be that they do not really wish to travel, or cannot come to terms with their travelling companions—but that can happen in the best of homes.

Some people look at our motorcaravan and say, 'However do you manage to live comfortably in such a small space?' The answer is to think simple; today everyone has become used to requiring more of everything and it is a relief when they find life in a motorcaravan enables them to have a very happy existence without so much clutter. Forget all about the requirements of living in a house; being in a motorcaravan is a different way of life. There is absolutely no need to be scruffy, dirty or deprived.

I recall that once we were in Spain parked on the seafront at Fuengirola. A gentleman passing by stopped and asked if he could look inside our motorcaravan; he was amazed that we could be living in such a small space and obviously thoroughly happy. He asked if he could bring his wife to see us. Subsequently, over a cup of coffee, she said that they would like to buy a motorcaravan. Then she said, 'Mary, I only hope that after four months constant travelling, I too, can keep as smart as you.' If I can do it, so can others, probably much better. Incidentally, I was wearing a drip-dry trouser suit that was two years old.

Starting with clothes, wherever one is travelling, there are some basic requirements. All clothes need to be of the type that are made for easy laundering. We are fortunate these days that so many fabrics are man-made, light and ideal for travel. I suggest the minimum requirements would be:

1 rainproof topcoat and hat
1 scarf and pair of gloves
3 pairs of trousers or 3 skirts
3 shirts or blouses
2 pairs of walking shoes or boots
1 pair of sandals or canvas shoes
3 sets of underwear
2 thick woollen jumpers
2 sets of nightwear
swim suit and sunhat

Depending where one travels, the weather conditions and time in a motorcaravan, it is necessary to supplement the above list.

Remember, it is possible to launder and iron clothes at many campsites. These days most towns in Britain and abroad have launderettes and dry cleaners. My husband and I find that track suits are convenient garments to have when travelling. We will wear them if we are having a night in a public place (having sought permission), for somehow we feel more prepared to greet an early-morning visitor in our tracksuits rather than jazzy pyjamas. When going for a swim a track suit makes a convenient cover-up for the walk back to the motorcaravan. We also have a 'best kit', so that if we want to treat ourselves to dinner at a smart hotel, we have the appropriate evening wear. The addition of cotton tops, teeshirts and scarves can help to ring the changes and brighten an outfit. When we want to buy ourselves a souvenir, a new scarf is a useful reminder of a happy visit.

It is, sadly, unwise to travel with any really valuable jewellery, especially if it is a sentimental piece. Leave it in a safe deposit at home if no amount of insurance could replace it. However, do take lots of trinkets, if you like wearing them, or again, collect some souvenirs as you go on your travels. Regretfully, I had some jewellery stolen from a bag in a locked motorcaravan when in

Italy. Fortunately it was well insured with the AA Five Star Travel Service and they made a very fair and just compensation on our return home. At that time we were going along the coast and my husband spent a long time searching for some sea shells, which he patiently made into a necklace for me. It is now one of my special treasures.

Having decided what you are taking in the way of clothes, you must then pack them. So do have crease-resistant clothes as far as possible. If you are really efficient, put various items into plastic bags. I especially recommend that you pack 'his' and 'hers' separately so that there is no argument when you both have brown socks and there is only a slight difference in size. Pack your shoes in a canvas bag, then if they are a bit muddy or sandy, the mess is confined to the bag. You will need clothes pegs and line, perhaps two; it is surprising how easy it is to drive away from a site leaving the line left tied to two trees, or sometimes you may intend to return to a chosen spot only to find a better place the other side of town.

A first-aid kit must be included. We have a small emergency pack in the front of the motorcaravan and a more comprehensive medicine box in a locker. Face-wipe tissues (the ones impregnated with cologne are the most refreshing), talcum powder and deodorant keep us fresh even on the longest journey. Small towels are better for easy laundering. I sew a tab to the centre edge of each towel; this can be useful in the shower. Your toilet bag should have a handle. I prefer to use liquid soap gel; it is easier to manage than a bar of soap that keeps slipping to the floor. Taking a plastic bag can be helpful for your clothes when the shower cubicle is small.

You will need handy mending materials, extra buttons, zips for trousers, scissors, needles, safety pins and a tape measure. I always include some clean rags, as my husband has a constant requirement for them when servicing the motorcaravan. Teacloths and dishcloths need to be small for easy laundering. A plastic-covered clothes dryer, which hooks on to the side of the vehicle but folds flat, or hangs in the toilet compartment, is essential on sites where washing lines may not be strung between trees. We keep our sleeping bags in a patterned pillowcase. They keep clean for ages if they are hung out to air each day. Pillows can double for cushions when they have an extra washable cover.

When eating snack meals a small tray helps to keep clothes clean. When having a picnic in the countryside or on the beach, the tray is a great help in keeping the sand away from the food. String bags can be used for storing fruit and vegetables; if you use an S-bend hook they hang almost anywhere. I like to keep my bread in a cotton bag. When travelling in Europe one sees all the housewives out shopping with freshly laundered '*pain*' bags; it will need to be at least 30in (75cm) in length, with a draw-string at one end—especially useful for the crusty French loaves which are so crumbly and crisp.

Plastic containers for food and drink are essential; make sure the lids fit well. Abroad, where a lot of food in the markets is sold by weight and unwrapped, it is sensible to take your own container for spices, honey, rice, olives, etc; even fish is much easier to transport in a plastic container. We are amused to see that often pebbles are used to offset the weight of the container on market stalls. Bottles will be needed if you go to a bodega to buy wine from the huge containers or barrels. Some of the big hypermarkets sell loose wine too. In Devon and Somerset we have purchased cider from large wooden barrels in this way. Of course you have to find the farm with the cider apples first, not so easy down those Devon lanes.

The number of cooking utensils you use will depend on the size of your motorcaravan. I manage very well with one large frying pan with a lid, a small saucepan with lid and a pressure cooker. We have added a coffee pot on our travels, plus a gas lighter. If you have a larger vehicle with an oven, then you will need more equipment, which says a lot for smaller vans. It is surprising how often one meets people who have forgotten the tin opener or corkscrew. Cutlery and crockery are very much personal choice. Some will manage with one knife, fork and spoon, while life is miserable for other people if they do not have their fish knives and forks with them. A really good kitchen knife and chopping board are invaluable.

Most people like to have folding chairs for the beach or a picnic, or just outside the motorcaravan. Perhaps the existing table can be adapted; four screw-on legs may do the trick. Household equipment will vary enormously with the size of your vehicle. In the little car-camper type, a small plastic bowl or two will be useful for doing chores outside. You may need a bucket for your

Bedford Trailblazer during Christmas in the Austrian Tyrol (*F. Penfold*)

waste water; in the larger motorhomes there will be a waste-water tank fitted. If there is no refrigerator an insulated food box will be helpful.

Lighting can be smart table lamps, fluorescent lights, gas lights or the humble candle. The last should always be available and we use them frequently. They help to create a real atmosphere of relaxation to go along with that bottle of wine or cup of coffee.

A 'must' is a fire extinguisher. The big fires start as small ones. Fitted within reach, preferably near the exit, an extinguisher can stop a nasty accident. A fire blanket is better for fat fires.

A question often asked is, 'Whatever do you do in the motorcaravan when you are away, but not travelling?' Firstly I would say that we live normally, that is we still eat, sleep, take exercise and a lively interest in all that is going on around us. The latter is probably our main occupation. Most travellers are observant people and it is sensible to be so for security reasons as well as pleasure. Keeping fit is essential; this means some exercise and a healthy diet.

Going to new shops and meeting people will always be

interesting. Whilst out shopping there will be plenty to see—and photograph—besides churches and museums. Fortunately films can be developed very quickly now in most countries. Serious walkers will park their motorcaravans by a long seashore or some interesting hills or valleys. They will enjoy a good tramp, with binoculars, especially if they are bird watchers, botanists or country lovers.

The seashore can provide hours of pleasure, whether it be swimming, watching marine life, fishing or just shell collecting. We have caught mackerel in Scotland and sardines in Spain. In Agadir, Morocco, we collected tiny clams on the sandy beach, where they can only be found when the tide is going out. It takes ages to wash them free of sand but they make a delicious soup. Free meals are always fun—I remember those delicious wild raspberries we picked in Scotland.

I spend time when not travelling writing to my family and friends. With my letters I relive our experiences, good and bad. Recently I have started to record messages on tape and have found they arrive safely, if posted in a strong envelope, providing a vivid and often amusing souvenir. One hilarious evening was had in Spain when free parking near a quiet beach, and I was recording a message to my family. We had a routine visit from the Spanish police and having been invited in for a glass of vino they became interested in our recording. It ended in them adding to the recording, including a song.

Rainy days provide the opportunity for reading. We always set off on our travels with a wide selection of paperbacks. Most towns have second-hand book shops, also the charity shops like Oxfam, and sell or exchange books. Along the southern coast of Spain you can buy or exchange English books either at newsagents or campsites. Many a time we have been approached by a fellow camper with an armful of books for swapping; it is a friendly way to make a new acquaintance and to hear news and information.

One of the things we enjoy when the weather is bad is to make ourselves cosy and get out some game like canasta, chess or Scrabble; we get really absorbed, especially if the loser has to pay a forfeit. Knitting or sewing can be very relaxing after several days on the road and it is good to sit and think about all one has seen and experienced. Perhaps I will do some extra cooking, something that involves preparation that is too complicated to do en route.

When we are stationary for a while, my husband will service the motorcaravan—routine checks on tyres, batteries, oil, plugs, fan belt, water, locks, windscreen wipers and many other things. We keep a daily record, which includes things like servicing, mileage and petrol used. The weather is recorded, incidents on the road, people we have met, things that we have bought, prices, places of interest, all go down in our little book. So often we have been glad of this record and not having to rely on memory.

Listening to the radio helps to keep us in touch with the news. We very much enjoy listening to a play, as we sit in the cosy comfort of our home on wheels. The BBC World Service has some excellent programmes. Reception can vary from country to country and it is worthwhile to have a radio that has a wide-band shortwave.

Living in a motorcaravan, it is very helpful to have some sort of routine for doing essential chores. Sometimes it is beneficial if these duties are shared or swopped. Most men will want to do the car maintenance, but the lady of the outfit should at least know what should be done in the way of routine servicing, where the spare wheel is kept and how to top up the battery. In fact the more she knows and understands about the vehicle the better. What about the gas fitments or filling the liquid for the windscreen wipers? In the event of an emergency can she use the fire extinguisher?

Likewise, share the shopping expeditions. Discuss the shopping list, talk about menus, ask your partner for assistance with price conversions. And washing clothes is another chore that can easily be shared; it will get the jobs done faster and leave everyone free to do other things.

Retirement comes early to many people these days and having a motorcaravan is often the answer to their prayers. Perhaps they have grown-up children who have settled to their own interests. So then it is an ideal time to get out and about with a new sense of adventure. After years of responsibility and timekeeping, the sheer freedom of owning a home on wheels is a delight for many retired people.

I have met several couples abroad who, new to retirement, have had difficulty in adjusting. A mother, who is often a grandmother too, will suffer about being away from her family. Do forget the cost and make that quick phone call home for a reassuring chat.

For those who have had a full-time career this is a period of big adjustment; it will take time for them to unwind. They have to relax and realise that suddenly here is great freedom.

Naturally there is hesitation in buying something that has not been tried, so it could be an advantage to hire a motorcaravan for a short holiday. Maybe a friend would let you borrow his vehicle for a few days. It is a good idea to study motorcaravan magazines and learn about the different types.

Having made your purchase you should then experience short periods away in it. Think of the pleasure of going to visit friends to show off your new interest and how independent you will feel if they are short of space, for you can provide your own bedroom and also make your own early-morning tea so easily. With your motorcaravan you will be able to attend sports meetings, go to late-night shows, or the theatre, with no worry about long drives home or looking for a hotel room. Your faithful motorcaravan will provide you with the warmth and comfort of familiar things at all times. Maybe you have always wanted to visit the National Trust properties in Britain. Good friends of ours, now retired and ardent motorcaravanners, plan lengthy periods away from home, in their motorcaravan, visiting such places. No other way could it be so easy.

To begin your motorcaravan life without too much strain, it is sensible to make use of the campsites that are spread all around the country. Join one of the many clubs. Maybe you will enjoy going to a local rally, where you will find plenty of friendly folk glad to pass on their keenness and experience to you. If you have some query, often a letter to a motorcaravan magazine will provide you with an answer, or several, for the motorcaravan fraternity are helpful people.

Winter wandering

Winters abroad in a motorcaravan are becoming increasingly popular and something that can really be recommended. From my experience and confirmed by many fellow travellers ('winter wanderers' is a common name given to us) living abroad in a motorcaravan need not be more expensive than being at home; indeed it is often cheaper, with the added bonus of a pleasant climate. The choice of where to travel during the winter months is varied, depending on what and where your interests lie. Obviously the further one travels the greater the initial outlay for travel expenses. Our motorcaravanning friends who are regular winter travellers spend their time in different places, usually the south of France, south of Spain, Algarve (Portugal), Sicily, Morocco and the Canary Islands. In all those countries it is feasible to enjoy the winter months in a motorcaravan.

A number of motorcaravanners travel continually all the year. We once met an English couple who had sold their house and bought a large motorcaravan. For five years they had been travelling happily, most of the time following the sunshine. In their case they were free camping everywhere except when they came to England for two months to visit their family; then they used a campsite as their base.

We have happy memories of shared Christmas dinners on a beach near Agadir, Morocco; New Year's Eve parties at Puerto Rico in Gran Canaria shared with German, Dutch and Swiss motorcaravanners; canasta games by candlelight in Portugal; roast jacket potatoes over a bonfire high on a mountain plateau under a moonlit sky with a young Israeli, his Finnish wife and poodle puppy. That young couple in their small Mercedes motorcaravan subsequently drove from the Canary Islands to Upper Volta in central Africa to seek work. Since then they have made the journey to Finland and returned by sea and road to Africa, still in their motorcaravan, plus poodle.

It is wise to get a map of the area you wish to travel, look at the terrain, and read books to ascertain the climate and conditions in winter. Look for any mountain passes to see when they are closed and, if necessary, plan an alternative route. Get your travel documents together in good time (see Chapter 9). Write to the appropriate National Tourist Office in London for up-to-date information and travel regulations. They will generally send you, free of charge, a map and list of campsites plus tourist information on specific areas. Write again if you do not get the correct information the first time. Should you be having any special medication, see your doctor about taking prescriptions or medicine, also get advice about inoculations.

Remember to have your vehicle serviced and buy some spares in case of need in out-of-the-way places. Check that campsites are open at the time you are travelling. In winter, some camps abroad, although officially closed, will allow you to park and use the

Bedford Auto-Sleeper at Goodwood Racecourse, Sussex in February 1982 (*Mrs T. J. Smith*)

limited facilities. Perhaps looking at a package tour brochure will give you an idea of the place you would like to visit, also information on temperatures and surrounding scenery.

Plan your route, petrol costs and mileage. From September onwards most of the ferries crossing the English Channel will include an increasing number of winter wanderers with their motorcaravans, heading for southern Europe. There are many routes, with various detours which can be made avoiding high mountain passes, closed by snow from November onwards. It may prove wise to use a motorway, the extra cost being offset by being able to spend a night at one of the service stations or rest areas en route.

The car ferry from Plymouth to Santander in northern Spain, which takes twenty-four hours, can be used to avoid the road journey across France. To reach the Canary Islands it is necessary to go to Cadiz in the south west of Spain. During the winter this ferry sails every five days or so. In summer it is more frequent. It is a pleasant crossing taking about forty-eight hours. Write to Aucona, Compania Trasmediterranea, Ave. Ramon De Carranza, 26, Cadiz, for a timetable and current fares. Cabins are air conditioned, with wash basins; the ship has a cafeteria, restaurant, swimming pool and cinema. It will stop at Tenerife before going on to Gran Canaria, and the same line has inter-island car ferries. It should be noted that in winter only one campsite is open amongst all seven islands. Situated at Tauro in Gran Canaria, it is extremely popular over the Christmas period, so it could be necessary to free camp.

Campsites are improving all the time, unfortunately the costs are also rising. However, in the southern areas abroad most campsites are open during the winter months, and offer reduced rates for long-term campers. At present it is cheaper to camp in Portugal than in Spain. Campsites give a sense of security and ease, plus a feeling of belonging to a community. Free camping is for roamers who wish to enjoy a quiet spot or view without too many people around. Modern motorcaravans with their own toilets, showers and waste-water tanks, make it possible to stay in remote areas and places where there are no campsites. On the other hand, free camping puts an onus on the camper to make sure that he is not causing any inconvenience to the public, and that he does not despoil the countryside (see Chapter 8).

For just a weekend away, a week's journey, or six months continual living in our motorcaravan, each time we move off with all our own things well stowed behind us, we have a great sense of pleasure and anticipation. During our years of motorcaravanning, life has been enriched by the many friends we have made—and the freedom and independence that no other vehicle could give us. No matter which make, size or type of motorcaravan you own, it will give you an entirely different style of living!

11
Accessories, equipment and extras

A motorcaravan is one complete entity, which is why I always write it as one word. All other forms of camping rely upon two components, such as a car and trailer, a cycle and tent—even a backpacker must be separated from his rucksack before he can begin camping. For the purposes of this chapter, however, the vehicle and the home will be treated separately, though it should be kept in mind that they function as one and are often interrelated as, for instance, when the vehicle's generator charges the auxiliary battery which supplies domestic services and entertainment.

Vehicle

There are certain items of equipment which are extremely desirable, if not essential for the motorcar side of the outfit. I will put these first, gradually tailing off to options which have their uses if you can afford them.

At the very top of my list go mud grips, for sooner or later there is going to be a soggy pitch somewhere, or wet grass on which the wheels spin. Mud grip mats can be made or bought. A couple of pieces of stout diamond mesh (it is rather tougher than wire netting) will cope with most situations. The cut ends and edges should be bent over with pliers or a hammer so that they do not tear hands or tyres. They can be stored flat, in a stout plastic or canvas bag, in the bottom of a locker, but there is often room in the engine compartment. The purpose-made kits are better, some having two or three sections hinged together so that they pack small and flat, others being specially cast with teeth that really grip the soft ground. A rather inferior alternative, but easy to buy and cut to shape, can be found in garden shops in the form of stout plastic netting, of about 2in (5cm) mesh. Plastic has a built-in slip factor when wet, so it is not ideal but better than nothing. Tie a long piece of string to each grip and, in use, secure the other end to a bumper. Then, when the grips have got the vehicle going, you drive right away from the mire, towing them behind.

Such mats could involve complications with front-wheel drive vehicles (unless you reverse out); most have low floors and the temporary tracks could become entangled underneath somewhere. The alternative to a mat is a wheel grip. Unlike complete tyre chains which are used for driving on snow or ice, wheel grips are simple little clamps which encircle the tyres radially. Often one per tyre is sufficient to get the vehicle moving. Before buying, look carefully at the wheels and tyre size of your particular vehicle. Some types sold for cars might not be large enough; practically all of them have to be wrapped around and secured, so holes in the wheels are essential. The vehicle should be driven slowly and the grips removed before motoring on the road.

Jump leads should be in the tool box, for starting difficulties are not unknown among motorcaravanners who park overnight on grass heavy with dew. I have even started my motorcaravan by connecting the secondary battery to the primary, when the latter was nearing the end of its useful life. Beware of buying low-priced leads in a high-street accessory shop. Cheap leads have an aluminium core; it is not as good a conductor as copper. The core should be really thick, too, for it has to bear a terrific current. When buying, look at several samples. The thickness of the core can be seen at the point where the cable is connected to the crocodile clip. A thin core will offer too much resistance and heat up like an electric fire, which means that the precious electricity is being dissipated in heat instead of flowing freely from battery to battery. Before using jump leads for the first time, do study the instructions. They are simple enough, but connecting a positive terminal to a negative could necessitate very expensive repairs.

An aerosol of water-repellent lubricant is another aid to starting under difficult conditions. Plug leads and distributor cap are first wiped clean, then sprayed—before retiring for the night if you remember it. It often helps to remove the distributor cap and dry out the interior with a clean soft rag or piece of kitchen towel. The increasing popularity of contactless electronic ignition fitted as original equipment will eventually dispose of this particular chore.

As an aside, if starting troubles persist, something should be done about it. The mobile tune-up services are often better at curing hidden faults than conventional garages, for the operators are specialists and have the back-up of electronic diagnosis equipment. What is more, you can watch the work in progress.

156

Spares for the vehicle can be kept to a minimum or augmented as you see fit. It is worth chatting with the foreman of the local agents for your vehicle; he will know what is most likely to give trouble. Owners of older, air-cooled Volkswagens were always recommended to carry a spare fan belt, for instance, though most ordinary motors could get by with the universal replacement fan belt sold by accessory shops. It is cut to length and joined after being threaded around the pulleys, which procedure saves a lot of dismantling on awkward engines. Some motorists have reported that a nylon stocking, tightly knotted, makes a replacement capable of getting the fan and water pump going well enough to allow several miles of motoring.

If you carry only minimum spares as a general rule, it is advisable to augment the stock when travelling abroad, especially if the vehicle is likely to be an uncommon one overseas. The local agents for the make will advise and I have found mine to be willing to make up a pack on sale or return. There was no handling charge, probably because I have been a good customer over the years. The motoring organisations offer a similar service, for which there is a charge.

It is essential to carry spare fuses and a set of light bulbs. The latter is obligatory in certain continental countries and advisable everywhere. You are committing an offence anywhere by driving with a vehicle light not working but if a box of spare bulbs can be produced when you are stopped, you will probably be let off the hook.

Tools are up to you and your inclination and ability. As the vehicle is a caravan, it makes sense to carry, in addition to the usual basic set of spanners, a small kit of handyman tools and a few self-tapping screws for running repairs to the 'home' as well as the car. A 12V electric drill is more compact than a wheel brace, will reach awkward spots, and saves a lot of effort. I always carry two jacks. As in so many commercial vans, my spare wheel is tucked inaccessibly underneath. It is heavy, and extremely difficult to manipulate when lying on one's back. A scissors jack will take the weight. The vehicle's bottle jack must be placed under the rear axle. When in use, it compresses the road springs and the wheel cannot be removed because the side skirt gets in the way. The second jack will give enough extra lift to the body to allow it to be withdrawn. An axle stand would serve the same purpose, plus a

A long wheelbrace gives plenty of leverage for stubborn wheel nuts

number of packing pieces to raise the jack during the second lifting operation. Some vehicles do not pose such difficulties, having sensible jacking points beneath the bodies. They lift the body clear of the wheel, then the wheel clear of the ground. It is a point worth looking into at home, on a fine day, before you get a puncture. The packing pieces which I put beneath the jack are just offcuts of timber, hard enough not to warp or split under pressure. They are also used to chock wheels when jacking and as levelling ramps when camping on sloping or uneven ground.

A tow rope can be coiled away in an odd corner somewhere. It could enable another motorist to get you out of trouble or vice versa. If you are stuck in a foreign country and do not speak the language, a rope held up and a pleading look will make the need obvious. As with jump leads, do not be tempted to go for the cheapest. A loaded motorcaravan can be a fair weight and something designed to retrieve a Mini could snap under the strain. It is a little more bulky, but a plastic-covered wire rope is the most reliable, provided it is padded with rag if taken round a sharp projection. Surprisingly, perhaps, the decorative nylon chain sold by some hardware and garden shops is really tough. I tested a length once, towing another motorcaravan, and it only snapped when the towed vehicle was deliberately braked hard. We used the largest size, with about $2\frac{1}{2}$in (6cm) links.

Among the other bits and pieces carried in the car part of my motorcaravan are a reserve supply of petrol, a flashing beacon torch and a warning triangle. Chapter 9 illustrates the desirability of the last two. I have never had to use the reserve petrol supply, except for cleaning purposes, but have more than once been able to help others out of trouble. Do not be tempted to use an old oil can for the petrol. It is not safe, will smell and could be illegal. Some of the latest petrol cans are safe from fire and explosion, do not leak fuel or fumes and come with extension pipes for awkward filler orifices.

LIGHTS

The remainder of the motoring equipment listed here is of the 'bolt-on' type, none of it essential but a lot of it desirable.

After reading of some horrible pile-ups on motorways, I now think a rear foglamp is a very necessary addition (the latest vehicles are so fitted, anyway). I also applaud the habit adopted by some motorway drivers of switching on hazard flashers as soon as an incident or obstruction is spotted ahead and usually long before the vehicle has come to a stop. It serves to alert the probably dreaming drivers behind. The law says that hazard flashers may be used only when the vehicle is stationary, but I doubt if any court would convict a motorist for using them in the above circumstances. The law also says that there must be some indication to a driver that the rear foglamp is switched on; this is usually accomplished by an illuminated switch. A retro-fitted rear foglamp should bear an E-mark.

The illuminated switch will also be needed if you decide to fit a reversing lamp, for few commercial vehicles come with them built in or with the necessary gearbox connection for automatic operation. It is possible to buy a reversing lamp with a red cover in the form of a clip-on lens so that it can double as a fog lamp. I do not think this is a very good idea, having tried it. The thing is seldom in the right mode when it is needed.

SOUND-PROOFING

Noise can make long journeys tiring and the commercial vehicles on which most motorcaravans are based suffer from more than their fair share. With one or two honourable exceptions, in-cab sound levels have been higher than those of comparable cars. Only recently have vehicle manufacturers started fitting special 'hush packs' as original equipment. As a consequence, motorcaravanners have perforce become very interested in add-on soundproofing. Kits are made for the front ends of most popular vans. They consist of heavy felt or substitute, anti-vibration pads and adhesive. The bits can be bought separately in good motor-accessory shops and take a day or more to install. Wear old clothes, and ascertain the solvent for the adhesive before beginning operations. Pads of felt or compressed-foam pieces can be used to treat the remainder of the caravan. Just put it everywhere — under the carpet, in cupboards, behind panels — the more the better. There will be *some* improvement, but that is all. For best results, the work needs to be done by an expert. People who convert run-of-mill production-line cars into expensive 'specials' are the ones to seek out, if you have the money to spare.

After several DIY attempts at soundproofing, I have found that treatment to cab floor, wheel arches and underside of the bonnet or engine cover lid brings most rapid results without undue strain. One thing soundproofing kits never seem to include is a tube of mastic or non-setting adhesive for sealing all the little gaps around cables (and holes where cables might go) which run from cab to engine compartment. A great deal of engine noise creeps through there. It must be non-setting adhesive so that cables can be renewed or flex as necessary. Bath caulk seems to work.

An electric radiator fan appears to do more towards noise reduction than towards the fuel economy so often claimed. It switches itself on only when the engine gets too hot and 90 per cent of the time it seems not to be needed on front-engine vehicles. The blades of the ordinary belt-driven fan are removed and fitting the electric one is usually a bolt-on operation. If the vehicle has a rear or in-cab engine, consult the fan makers before buying. Electric fans are also used, as a supplement to the original, on vehicles which suffer from overheating. They are popular among trailer caravanners (which bracket includes a few motorcaravanners) who storm alpine passes.

Overdrive saves fuel and decreases noise and wear and tear on both vehicle and occupants. It is best ordered factory-fitted with a new vehicle. Although there are some bolt-on kits approved by the vehicle manufacturers, retrospective fitting will involve either stripping the gearbox or shortening and rebalancing the prop shaft. The resultant bill is likely to be in the region of £400 or more. This puts a high price on quietness and fuel economy (which is roughly of the order of 5 per cent). Knowledgeable DIY mechanics have spent far less than this by searching breakers' yards and tackling the work themselves.

OFF-ROAD MOTORING

Motorcaravanners who do a lot of off-road motoring will probably go for a four-wheel-drive vehicle. There is a constant but limited market for conversions of the famous Land Rover but the end result is a rather cramped caravan and there are now other options available. Four-wheel-drive conversion of an ordinary delivery van is possible but expensive. A limited slip or lockable differential would satisfy the needs of the majority of away-from-it-all motorcaravanners. Such conversions can usually be carried out in a day. Most of us get stuck in the mud when one driven wheel spins violently, because the differential gear is doing its stuff. The amount of torque going to the non-spinning wheel is so slight as to be insufficient to turn it. Locking the differential or limiting its slip would restore traction to two wheels, and make the vehicle drivable in all but the most daunting conditions.

A winch, mounted ahead of the engine on a substantial bracket which replaces the bumper bar, is another bolt-on alternative which off-road motorcaravanners might consider. Being electrically operated, it is simple to fit. If you are stuck, you dismount and walk forward to firm ground, unwinding the rope from the drum of the winch as you go. The end is attached to a tree or a stake driven into the ground. Switch on and winch yourself out of the mire.

'Home'

As the motorcaravan is a home from home, the number of extras that can be added to it is virtually limitless. I will begin with some items that, from experience, I would not want to be without. The less essential ones will come later.

A fire extinguisher is an *essential* item of equipment

A fire extinguisher and/or blanket should be regarded as part of the standard equipment, not as an extra. Aerosol extinguishers have a limited life and should be renewed every few years. British Standards or Fire Office approved dry powder extinguishers are recommended, and should be of at least 1kg capacity. Halon gas extinguishers, though effective, can be dangerous when used in confined spaces. A second extinguisher should, ideally, be supplied for the engine compartment. Many motorcaravanners settle for an extinguisher in the cab and a fire blanket near the cooker.

WATER, CHEMICAL CLOSETS, ETC

Some motorcaravans carry their fresh-water supplies in portable containers which can be removed for filling; others have built-in tanks, either beneath a seat or slung in a cradle under the floor. In this case, a water carrier of some sort is essential for filling the tank. Two small ones are easier to store and carry than one large. I also carry a short length of drinking-water hose and a universal tap fitting for those occasions when the motorcaravan can be driven close to the tap. Two people are then needed, one at the tap and one at the filler. If the filler orifice is located in the side of the vehicle, the water porter will need a spout. If it is high off the ground, it is a job to lift the container and pour. Then an electric submersible pump is a boon. For suggestions, see Chapter 6.

The submersible pump can be put to other uses, such as washing sand off feet before entering the caravan, after a visit to the beach. With a shower rose and a container filled with warm water, you can have a showerbath in, perhaps, the toilet tent. If the motorcaravan has a toilet compartment not equipped for showering, shower trays can be bought, or a large bowl used. When travelling, the bowl becomes a storage tray in a locker or cupboard.

Annexes were dealt with in Chapter 7. One such, or a toilet tent, is invaluable if the motorcaravan is small or number of occupants large. A toilet tent can on occasion be useful even in a coachbuilt fitted with a toilet compartment; it relieves pressure on the inevitably restricted space in the caravan and provides a temporary home for damp towels and clothes or muddy boots.

A spare gas container is highly desirable. Even with the gauges now beginning to come on to the market you can never be exactly sure when the gas is going to run out—except that it will be at a most inconvenient time. Many caravanners carry a small, single burner stove and a throwaway cartridge, which can quickly be pressed into use. It is a life saver in the unlikely event of a fault developing in the gas system.

Two-piece chemical closets make an essential chore that much easier

Chemical-closet uses and management were covered in Chapter 7. This is the place to describe the various types, beginning with the simplest, which is a small folding seat with a plastic bag beneath—rather unattractive and suitable only for young chidren. These closets are sold by some baby shops and are probably more practicable than the usual potty, because the bag can be sealed until a disposal point is reached.

The familiar and much unloved old 'Elsan' still exists, though in a somewhat more pleasing shape and made of colourful plastics rather than sheet metal. Other manufacturers supply similar products, which are essentially large buckets with seats and lids. Some have inner containers. A sealing lid is essential for people on the move.

The chemical closets described in the following paragraphs are superior (though a little more complicated) in that there is a bowl or pan which hides contents from the user, rather like the loo at home. These do not need sealing lids.

For a long time, I preferred the recirculating type because it uses no extra water and should therefore require less frequent servicing. The effluent in the container, rendered harmless by the chemical closet fluid (which must, in all cases, be added), is recirculated through a filter by a pump as flushing water. It is fine, if you stay in one place and effluent can settle. Driving around, it all gets stirred up, the filter tends to clog and the flushing water bears little bits of solid matter. The Americans make a superior model with an electric pump for the flush which, on trial, gave no trouble. It was also coupled to a holding tank which gave two of us complete independence for more than a week.

Far and away the most popular system with motorcaravanners is the two-piece closet with fresh-water tank. The lower half is the holding tank for effluent, the upper incorporates seat, pan and a supply of water. After each use, the pan is flushed (using a hand or, occasionally, electric pump) and disgorged into the tank below by pulling a lever. When the holding tank is full, it is detached and carried to the disposal point. As it is the size and shape of an ordinary water container, it is fairly easy to carry, depending on how full it has become. A simpler, and cheaper, version of the two-piece chemical closet is all in one. It works in just the same way, but the whole thing must be taken to the disposal point for emptying.

As might be expected, the huge American motorhome market inspires development of new ideas. Most motorhomes built there have big tanks for holding sewage, which can be emptied at 'dump stations'. In effect, this means that the loo is the same as the one at home (except that flushing water is pumped, by hand or electrically) and the holding tank is merely a small cesspit. British campsites are gradually awakening to the need to provide dumping facilities for sewage. When one (or a convenient manhole) cannot be found, a full holding tank leaves the owner wishing he had a simple two-piece loo which could be emptied into any lavatory pan.

A word about chemical closet fluids. Most readily available in all caravan and camping shops are the various 'blue' fluids which are formaldehyde-based. These can safely be disposed of via any sewage outlet, for the fluid does not disturb the bacteria necessary to the functioning of septic tanks (on which many campsites rely). For this reason, the Caravan Club (along with other authorities) forbids the use of caustic-based fluids or powders. The latter can safely be disposed of in holes dug in waste ground—not always easy to find in crowded Britain—or via some (but not all) domestic lavatories.

Insulation and double glazing have already been mentioned. These desirable extras will allow use of the motorcaravan through more months of the year. A waste-water tank will permit use in more places, such as for a lunch stop in the car park after shopping at a supermarket. It is not always possible, or desirable, to place a bucket outside beneath the sink's waste outlet.

Both waste and fresh-water tanks can be fitted with water-level gauges. It is a fairly simple DIY operation and, although I have so far managed without one, I suppose that knowing how much water there is on board is nearly as important to the motorcarav-anner as the reading on the fuel gauge. Water gauges are usually electrical (see Chapter 6) but there has been a return to the old-fashioned method of a capillary tube running from the tank to the gauge. Contents are indicated by the position of a little ball floating on a column of liquid, like vintage petrol gauges.

It is advisable to have an alternative source of water if the main supply is in a tank. This is usually provided by a water porter kept filled but you might think it worth carrying a spare pump or installing a dual manual/electric pump. As faults can develop in the system for no apparent reason, I also carry a few hose clips and a short length of water hose, for running repairs.

ELECTRICAL DEVICES

Many motorcaravans, especially low-price converted vans, have the minimum number of interior lights, perhaps just one fluorescent. The tubes are now so reliable that it is hardly worth carrying a spare, which is fragile anyway and difficult to store. Better to install another fluorescent or a few spotlights in suitable positions. A filament lamp rated at 10W will consume less current than a standard 13W fluorescent. It gives out far less light, being by comparison inefficient, but there is enough for one person to read by at a distance of about 3ft. For this reason, my wife and I have small filament spot lamps above our pillows in bed. We can read or sleep without disturbing each other. A third, in the kitchen, is a standby, used mainly when we are listening to the radio, for our fluorescents produce a whistle on all wavelengths except VHF. Some lamps are run from the car's battery, others from the secondary (belt and braces principle again).

Most motorcaravanners will want a radio. In a small vehicle, it is sensible to save space by using the car's. Sometimes, however, the dashboard is just too difficult to reach from the caravan so, if there is not already a car radio fitted, it is worth trying to work out another position, perhaps by the side of one of the front seats. On one vehicle, we compromised by carrying a small portable radio and cassette player in the caravan and shunted its output through a pair of good speakers, wall-mounted, for reasonable repro-duction.

During long, dark evenings or on rainy days, a small television set comes into its own. Black and white models are not greedy for electricity and can be run safely from the car battery for an hour or two. Colour sets should draw their supply from the auxiliary battery. If this is not available, fit a voltage sensor; it will interrupt the supply while there is still enough charge in the battery for starting the car the next day. Regular television addicts are recommended to install a 12V socket, with a plug which cannot be reversed to give wrong polarity, and a permanent aerial. Some of the latest are omni-directional. When mounted on the roof they receive signals from any direction. Others can be remote controlled from inside the caravan. Tuning with two people is funny to observe, frustrating to do, with one person inside watching the picture and calling instructions to the aerial rigger outside.

Other electrical devices might include a fan. There are two types: free standing and extractors. A 12V free-standing fan will move the air about, can usually be placed anywhere and is held by suction feet. More expensive versions will oscillate, ie turn from side to side whilst working. They provide a welcome breeze in hot weather. Extractor fans are fitted to a wall, where they will draw unwanted heat or fumes from the kitchen area or toilet compartment. Cooker hoods in caravans usually have fans incorporated and often lights, too. A clear wall space is needed for mounting or they may sometimes be incorporated in a high-level wall cupboard. A superior type of extractor fan is reversible, and can be made to blow outside air into the caravan. The draught can be directed by adjustable louvres.

With all these appliances drawing electricity, plus perhaps a fan blower on the space heater, it is sensible to have a second battery, or perhaps a voltage sensor and the biggest possible vehicle battery. Some fantastic claims are made for several of the devices designed to supply caravan electrics. They are not always borne out in practice (see Chapter 6) and my advice is to consult a competent automobile electrician. Mains electricity is particularly of benefit to those who camp for several days without moving or in very cold weather (when batteries do not function at full efficiency). Again, the experts should be called upon. They can be found in the telephone directory and their knowledge can save a lot of expensive experimentation and the possibility of financial or fatal shock.

Away-from-it-all motorcaravanners should look at portable generators (a few top-price vehicles are already equipped). They come in all sizes, suitable for running anything from a television to a microwave oven, or they can just be used for charging batteries. Many site owners will not allow the use of generators. Nobody has yet produced a silent model, though some are quiet enough if you do not park close to others.

REFRIGERATORS

A refrigerator can, according to the majority opinion, be classed as a desirable extra. I have only left it until now because most modern motorcaravans are already equipped. Gas is the usual source of power, with 12V electricity when the vehicle is running or mains on site when available. A gas-only refrigerator can be fitted with 12V supply fairly easily; kits and instructions are supplied by the makers.

Gas refrigerators function on the absorption principle—they need heat to work the heat exchanger. When that heat is supplied by a 12V element, consumption is in the order of 8A/hour. The car's alternator can accommodate that when running, but the battery would soon be exhausted when stationary.

Compressor refrigerators have a motor (like domestic models) and consume half that amount of 12V electricity when they are running. Except in unfavourable conditions, they are unlikely to be running all the time, being thermostatically controlled. So their use in a motorcaravan is feasible. They have not really caught on because of high initial cost and the need for a second battery for more than overnight use when the vehicle is not moving. Unlike gas refrigerators, compressor models do not need accurate levelling, exude no fumes and pose no fire risk. If they were in more general use, the price might come down. On the other hand, if the price were competitive, they might be fitted more often as original equipment.

There are some interesting variations on electric refrigerators. A British manufacturer sells a kit for converting any cupboard into a cold box. One small model from Japan has an incorporated transformer, and can be plugged into mains electricity and used as a freezer when it is not required for camping purposes. Space-age technology has developed the Peltier principle, which relies on heat transference between two dissimilar metals. The little box can therefore be employed to cool wine or heat soup. At least one traveller has, to my knowledge, accidentally mulled his wine.

OVENS

If a cupboard can be spared, a gas oven can be fitted. Alternatively, if there is wall space, an oven or grill may be sited at eye level—an 'optional extra' on many imported luxury motorcaravans which, oddly, come with just two gas rings. An oven should not be used for heating the caravan in normal circumstances but the Americans have developed one which is externally vented and incorporates a fan for blown-air space heating. It is not available at

168

time of writing but is such a good idea that it must come back.

If there is no room, or little spare cash, a folding oven is sold by camping shops. It is placed on top of the gas ring and takes up little space when not in use. It is also worth searching caravan and hardware shops for dry-fry pans and waterless cookers. Many caravan cooks rely upon the pressure cooker. In general, it is fair to say that purpose-made pots and pans for campers are cheap and nasty, with detachable handles that fall off at the most inconvenient time. My wife insists on space being found for a nesting set of ordinary, non-stick domestic pans.

Still on the cooking front, outdoor barbecues are all the rage in Europe and America, though some British site owners will not permit their use. Charcoal was originally the only fuel, now there are gas-fired models, some of which have permanent ceramic elements which, it is claimed, neither wear out nor need cleaning.

STEADIES

Owners of larger motorhomes are sometimes bothered by the way the caravan rocks on site as people move about within. Rear steadies can be fitted, of the type seen on trailer caravans. They are wound down with a wheelbrace or can be electrically operated by pressing a button located inside somewhere. Either type may be locked when down, the former with a padlock, the latter with an ignition key, when they are transformed into an effective theft-deterrent. The Americans make sets of jacks which are bolted to the chassis. Pressing a button automatically renders the vehicle level and thief proof.

Security

This brings us logically to the final part of the chapter. With all that valuable equipment inside, not to mention the vehicle itself, thieves and 'house breakers' have got to be deterred. If a 'ringer' (a professional) is after your vehicle, there is not a lot you can do about it. He will have studied both your habits and those of the motorcaravan and have developed a fairly foolproof plan of action. But motorcaravans, unlike popular cars and even trailer caravans, do not often attract the professional at present. They offer however, an enticing prospect to the opportunist. So you need protection against the vehicle being driven away and unauthorised entry. Many anti-theft devices provide both.

They fall into a few distinct groups. A rocking pendulum senses unauthorised movement and can be adjusted so that the wind and bow waves from passing vehicles do not set it off. Current breaking or current making alarms are operated by hidden switches in doors and windows or by pressure mats. Another device measures any variation in battery voltage caused, for example, by a door being opened and operating the courtesy lamp. Some are elaborate electronic door keys on which a number known only to the owner is punched out. Most of these alarms will set off a siren or hooter, which you hope will deter further tampering. One sends a radio signal to the owner, who carries a 'bleeper' like the hospital doctors in television soap operas. As the Post Office will not license the system, it is *probably* illegal to use it, but it is the thief who will be setting it off.

As a first and easy step, I suggest a visual deterrent, like the stick that locks steering wheel to clutch or brake pedal, or the registration number etched on all windows. A sticker proclaiming that an anti-theft device has been fitted (even if it has not) might have some deterrent value.

You have only to watch a policeman about to drive away an illegally parked car to gauge how easy it is to those with the know-how. Though car locks are fairly ineffective, some of those fitted to the doors of coachbuilt motorcaravans are virtually useless. Any coachbuilder or body repairer will be able to fit high-security locks to all doors and a good ironmonger will have a stock of window locks. Spend a few minutes walking around your locked vehicle, trying to imagine how you would get in without a key. Then take appropriate measures, not forgetting the vulnerable-to-vandals fuel and water filling points and gas bottle locker. Then keep your fingers crossed.

12
Care of the motorcaravan

This will be the shortest chapter, for a motorcaravan is not difficult to look after, though it appreciates a little loving care. If well cared for, your motorcaravan will serve you for many years and open up a whole new way of life.

Vehicle

The vehicle, being based upon a commercial chassis, is tough, designed for rough treatment. It does not need a garage—I believe that most vehicles are better off in the open, subject to free circulation of air, rather than an enclosed garage where condensation collects. A car port is probably favourite.

This is not the place to give precise instructions about vehicle maintenance. If you do your own servicing and repairs, there are books a-plenty, from drivers' handbooks to comprehensive workshop manuals. Most popular seem to be the Haynes manuals sold in motor accessory shops. They are a good half-way house for the average mechanic but are unlikely to guide you through the more ambitious repairs and replacements. For that, the workshop manual published by the vehicle makers will be needed—unless you happen to own a pre-1978 air-cooled Volkswagen, when the American *How to Keep Your Volkswagen Alive* (Selpress Books, last revised 1979) will provide both amusing and instructive reading.

People who take their vehicles to a local garage for servicing still need to know a little more than the average motorist. Whatever kind of vehicle is owned, it is advisable to keep an eye on oil, water and battery levels and to check tyre pressures occasionally, when they are cool and with your own gauge. Do not forget the spare. The garage probably will, though it is listed on the service schedule. Let them know you are in the habit of checking up on their work.

Other easy chores that should be carried out periodically include inspection of tyre walls (both sides) and treads, removing flints and pieces of broken glass. If front treads show uneven wear, have steering alignment checked. Feel the radiator and heater hoses; if there is any sign of sponginess, have them replaced. Pull up floor carpets or mats after rain or washing, to ensure that water is not penetrating somewhere (a symptom is a musty smell).

Although it is not the purpose of this book to provide an alternative to an instruction manual, the problem of tyre pressures for motorcaravans is a recurring one. Few motorcaravan manufacturers make any recommendations and the vehicle's instruction book probably relates to commercial loads. In the absence of any other guidance, correct procedure is to weigh the vehicle, loaded as for touring, at front and rear separately. Then write to the tyre manufacturer for guidance.

Perhaps the most important item of maintenance is the regular hose-down of the underside, especially after frost when corrosive salt may have been used on the roads. All traces of mud must be removed, for mud holds dampness and encourages rust. A clean chassis will soon be bone dry. As for the various undersealing compounds and application services, believe what you will. Some people swear by certain brands. Steam cleaning and drying before application is essential, for any moisture trapped beneath a coat subsequently applied will remain there, quietly doing its damage. If you can face it, a thorough cleaning followed by a twice yearly application of used engine oil costs nothing but time.

Motorcaravans have more ground clearance than most cars. This is fortunate, making it possible for the owner to inspect the underside without recourse to ramps or axle stands. (Never crawl beneath a vehicle which is merely jacked up and resist the temptation to prop it up on bricks or paving slabs, which could crumble. Chock the wheels, too, when you are down under.) What to look for underneath will depend on the motorcaravan. Examine water and waste tanks and gas-bottle cradles for secure attachment and go over all water and gas pipes, checking that joints are tight and that nothing is chafing. It will do no harm to confirm that brake lines are not rubbing against any caravan equipment that has been slung beneath and that, if screws project through the floor (as they often do) they are not dangerously close to brake hoses, petrol lines or electric cables. Give the screws a squirt of rust inhibitor. It is really a matter of looking around to see that all is well. Do not hurry the job; make yourself comfortable with an old cushion to support the head. I once spotted, just in time, a plastic petrol pipe which had worn wafer-thin by rubbing against the exhaust pipe because a clip had come adrift. That was bad design on the part of the vehicle builders.

Wash the outside of the vehicle once a week if you can stand it. If you have a hose, fit a soft brush to it, on an extension arm if the vehicle is high. If there is no hose, use a soft brush on a stick and plenty of water. Brushes get into crannies and float the dirt off. A sponge is inclined to rub it in. If the vehicle is a high one, use a pair of steps. Do not be tempted to use harsh treatment to remove grime and bird droppings from a glass fibre roof. It scratches easily. A repeated application of fairly hot water usually does the trick. In stubborn cases a jelly hand cleaner can work wonders without scratching. The same stuff helps stubborn windows to slide. Treat acrylic caravan windows very gently, they, too, easily scratch. Other outside jobs will include preservation of chrome trimmings and aluminium window surrounds. Car shops will supply a suitable cleaner. Corroded aluminium may need one fairly harsh treatment with fine wire wool but be careful not to scratch surrounding paint work.

Oil door locks and hinges occasionally and sparingly. Excess oil collects dirt and gets on clothes. Use an aerosol lock de-icer in winter. Precision locks such as a Yale (I have fitted a double locking latch to the back door) should be lubricated with graphite; oil can gum the works.

Interior
Inside, it is all very much like looking after the home. The great enemy is dampness. Look for tell-tale staining that denotes a leaking roof or joint in a wall. It could involve stripping off interior panelling and drying out before repair. Some coachbuilt caravans are particularly prone. There should be no dampness inside. We reckon to leave sleeping bags and bedding in our motorcaravan throughout the year, never knowing when they will be needed. They are given an occasional airing. When removed in winter, they will feel cold but not damp.

Cupboards beneath sinks often develop damp patches caused by careless plumbing of water and waste pipes. It is a matter of checking all the joints and tightening hose clips, using a drop of non-setting sealant or bath caulk in stubborn cases. The corrugated hose often used for waste pipes will not stand too many re-tightenings. The mangled end must be cut off or the whole pipe replaced. It will need renewing after two or three years anyway.

In-line water filters have a limited life. Yearly replacement is usually the rule. A gas refrigerator will need a service every year, at least (more frequently if flues soot up rapidly). The maker's instruction leaflet will detail the procedure but is unlikely to tell you how to remove the thing in the first place. It means searching for half-hidden screws in nearby panels, or a phone call to the motorcaravan manufacturer for advice. If the job proves daunting, local bottled-gas service centres are listed in the telephone directory. Some service engineers will do the whole job, removing and replacing the brute, and charging appropriately. Others require the owner to remove the refrigerator, in which case it is worth asking local caravan dealers if they can cope. Gas plumbing should be tested for leaks and other appliances given the once-over at the same time, though it is fair to say that none requires the amount of attention demanded by the refrigerator. All-electric compressor or Peltier principle refrigerators are usually trouble free for years. Maintenance or repair is a job for the makers if it ever becomes necessary.

If the caravan is wired for mains electricity, that should have a yearly safety check by a qualified electrical engineer. This is particularly necessary if the system incorporates a contact breaker or polarity sensing device. No apology is offered for repetition of the caution: mains electricity can kill.

Furniture may be scuffed and need more than a polish. Find out first what it is made of. Veneered plywood can be rubbed down with glasspaper (gently, because the veneer is thin) and re-varnished or french polished (amateur kits are available from DIY shops and come with instructions) as appropriate. Chipboard may be faced with real wood veneer or a printed imitation. The latter cannot be repaired. Small marks may be disguised by darkening (eg with a felt pen) and polishing. If the damage is serious, the whole panel must be re-faced or completely replaced. The motorcaravan manufacturer may be able to supply a replacement door or panel from stock if the vehicle is not very old. It is worth trying.

Materials for reviving stainless steel sinks can be bought in hardware shops. The space beneath the grill is inaccessible in many motorcaravans. If you do not fancy dismantling the whole unit, the only alternative is a rag tied to a stick.

The rest will be normal domestic chores of cleaning and

polishing. A powerful vacuum cleaner will be invaluable, with extension hose for reaching into crannies (12V cleaners from car-accessory shops are alright for daily maintenance but the yearly spring-clean demands real suction).

Appendix 1

A motorcaravanner's dictionary

A-class (US) Motorhome built on a chassis, as distinct from chassis-cab, so that front seats form part of living area.

Acrylic sheet A 'plastic', clear or tinted, used in place of safety glass for some side and rear windows, single or double glazed.

Algae Minute primitive plants which can grow in water systems when light is not excluded.

Annexe A tent which extends the living area of a motorcaravan. May be attached or free-standing.

Articulated vehicle Half way between a trailer caravan and motorcaravan; the caravan body is attached to a pivot mounted on the tractor unit (usually a pickup truck).

Automotive gas Propane gas which propels a vehicle.

Auto-Sleeper Trade name sometimes erroneously describing any motorcaravan.

Awning A shelter attached to a motorcaravan. (An awning completely enclosed with side and end walls would be an annexe.)

Balanced flue heater Space or water heater where products of combustion are exhausted to exterior.

Black water Sewage.

Blocking diode One-way electrical 'valve' used in some dual-battery systems.

Brewers' hose Non-toxic polythene hose used in water systems.

BSI British Standards Institution, which makes recommendations for standards of manufacture, materials etc.

Butane A liquefied petroleum gas—will not vaporise at temperatures much below zero.

Camping car (US) A van converted to provide living accommodation.

Cant rail The curved part of the roof of a van, above the guttering.

Caravette Trade name sometimes erroneously describing any motorcaravan.

Car tax Tax levied on cars at point of sale, but not on commercial vehicles. A van made into a motorcaravan is liable for car tax.

Catalytic heater Gas heater with no flame; energy in the fuel is converted to heat by catalytic action.

CDV Car derived van.

Certificated location Small informal campsite for exclusive use of members of an organisation.

Chassis-cab Driving compartment on a chassis on which is mounted a coachbuilt body.

Chassis-scuttle Chassis, engine and front end only; usually the basis for A-class motorhome.

Chemical closet Container for human waste, usually portable. Contents are rendered innocuous by use of a chemical, usually formaldehyde-based.

Class A (US) See 'A-class'.

Coachbuilt Special body attached to a chassis-cab; does not necessarily imply conventional coachbuilding construction.

Compression fitting Joint in a gas or water pipe formed simply by tightening a nut.

Contact breaker Device which automatically breaks an electric circuit, eg in case of overload or short circuit.

Conversion Vehicle (normally commercial) converted into a motorcaravan.

Cradle Support, usually of steel, for spare wheel, gas bottle, water tank etc.

Demountable BSI recommend 'dismountable', see below.

Dismountable Caravan body which may be used either mounted on, or dismounted from a chassis-cab or flatbed truck.

Dormobile Trade name sometimes erroneously describing any motorcaravan.

Dump station Emptying point for sewage holding tank.

Effluent Contents of chemical closet or holding tank.

ELCB Earth leakage contact breaker: device for turning off mains electricity in case of faulty wiring or connection.

Elevating roof BSI recommends 'rising roof', see below.

Extractor fan Electrically powered fan (usually 12V) for extraction of stale air.

Faucet Tap which delivers water supply to sink or basin. May be fitted with shut-off valve.

Fibreglass Trade name for glass fibre.

Fifth wheeler (US) Articulated caravan.

Flame failure device Cuts off gas supply to an appliance if flame is extinguished.

Flatbed truck Cab and flat load area for a dismountable caravan.

Free camping Camping at a place which is not a recognised campsite.

Furnace (US) Gas space heater which blows warm air through ducts.

Gas bottle Container for butane or propane gas, exchangeable when empty.

Gas cartridge Small disposable gas container.

Gas cylinder Same as gas bottle.

Gas regulator Device which reduces pressure of gas in container to a constant reading.

Gas tank LPG (liquefied petroleum gas) container (usually propane) permanently installed in motorcaravan, for vehicle propulsion and/or domestic appliances.

Gas tank (US) Petrol tank.

Generator (1) Portable or fixed petrol or diesel auxiliary motor supplying electric current. (2) Dynamo or alternator on vehicle.

Glass fibre Form of GRP, see below.

Grey water (US) Waste water which is not sewage.

Grommet Rubber or plastic washer which lines a hole through which a cable passes — prevents chafing.

GRP Glass reinforced plastic: used for roofs and occasionally whole bodies. Useful DIY material for minor repairs.

Heat exchanger water tanks Use unwanted engine heat to supply hot water for the caravan.

Holding tank (US) A mobile cesspit carried on the vehicle. Needs a dump station for emptying.

Hook-up Usually mains electricity taken to the motorcaravan at a campsite. Unusually, except in America, also connection of mains water and drainage.

Instantaneous water heater Gas appliance which heats water as it passes through.

Jump leads Heavy electric cables used to connect temporarily the battery of one vehicle to another.

KD furniture 'Knock down' furniture kit which is assembled by the buyer.

Levelling jacks Attached to chassis, they allow a motorcaravan to be levelled on sloping or uneven ground.

Levelling ramps Usually wooden boards, on to which the motorcaravan is driven to make it level.

Light delivery van Commercial van of about 1 ton load capacity, basis for majority of motorcaravan conversions.

Luton Compartment above cab, used for storage or as a bed.

Motorcaravan Self-propelled caravan.

Motorhome Large motorcaravan, fully equipped. (Loosely: any motorcaravan.)

Motorised caravan Motorcaravan.

Mud mats Metal or plastic mats placed beneath driving wheels to provide grip.

Neoprene hose Flexible hose connecting gas container to gas plumbing.

Nibbler Electric tool for cutting sheet metal.

Non-return valve Prevents water in plumbing system draining back to storage tank.

Non-toxic hose Flexible hose used for drinking water supplies.

Odometer Mileage (or distance) recorder.

ohc Overhead camshaft and valves.

ohv Overhead valves.

Olive Copper or brass filler which makes compression joints gas-tight.

One-off Unique or special; not one of many similar models.

Panel van Light delivery van, popular as basis for motorcaravan conversion.

Pickup truck Integral cab and truck body produced by vehicle manufacturer.

Pitch Part of a campsite on which one caravan is parked.

Pitch marker Means of indicating that a pitch is reserved for an absent motorcaravan, eg vehicle's registration number or tent pegs and tape.

PK screws Self-tapping screws, see below.

Plastolene Trade name for material commonly used for flexible walls of rising roofs.

Polarity tester Device for ensuring that mains electric hook-up is right way round.

Polythene hose Clear or black—commonly used for water systems in motorcaravans.

Power pack 12V battery in a case, which may be charged by vehicle or mains electricity, used to power motorcaravan's electric services.

Private conversion One-off motorcaravan conversion by a private individual.

Propane A liquefied petroleum gas which vaporises at lower temperatures than butane.

Rally Meeting of motorcaravans, usually organised by a club.

Relay Automatic switch which isolates car battery from second battery.

Rig (US) Any sort of home on wheels.

Rising roof Roof which is raised to provide standing room in a motorcaravan.

Roof cap The solid, top part of a rising roof.

Rough camping Wild or free camping.

RV (US) Recreation vehicle—usually applied to a motorhome or car camper.

Self-priming water pump Draws water from a lower level.

Self-tapping screws Cut their own thread when driven into a pilot hole in metal.

Semi-trailer Articulated vehicle.

Sewage Contents of chemical closet or holding tank—term not normally applied to water from sink or wash basin.

Site Location where motorcaravans may park overnight or longer.

Solar control film Thin transparent film applied to windows to reduce heat transference.

'Special' Motorcaravan purpose-built or equipped to the owner's specification.

Steadies Legs, manually or power operated, to prevent motorcaravan rocking on springs when parked.

Storage water heater Warms a quantity of water in a container.

Submersible water pump Electric pump placed in water container.

Template Guide for cutting or drilling.

Tractor (unit) The motorised part of an articulated vehicle.

Trim, trimming Decorative strip applied over joins or at edges of panels.

Tyre chains Chains fastened to wheels to provide traction on snow or ice.

VAT Value added tax: charged on value of motorcaravans and equipment therein after car tax has been assessed.

Voltage sensor Device which switches off electrical supply when battery voltage drops to a pre-set level. Prevents car battery being exhausted by caravan electrics.

Water filter Device for filtering solid matter from water supply, also used erroneously to describe water purifier.

Water purifier Device for making contaminated water fit to drink. Often contains a water filter.

Wheel grips Straps fastened radially around driving wheels to provide traction on grass or mud. Should not be used as tyre chains on snow or ice.

Wild camping Camping in remote places, often synonymous with free camping and rough camping.

Appendix 2

The principal motorcaravan manufacturers

Autohomes (UK) Ltd, 59 Old Wareham Road, Poole, Dorset.
  Rising roofs and coachbuilts. Bedford, Fiat, Talbot, VW.
Auto-Sleepers Ltd, Orchard Works, Willersey, Broadway, Worcs.
  Rising roofs, high tops and coachbuilts. Bedford, Ford,
  Renault, Sherpa, Talbot, VW.
Auto-Trail Ltd, Beels Road, Kiln Lane, Stallingborough, Grimsby.
  Coachbuilts. Bedford, Mercedes, Peugeot.
Canterbury Conversions, South Essex Motors (Basildon) Ltd,
  Cherrydown East, Basildon, Essex.
  Rising roofs and high tops. Bedford, Ford.
Carawagon Ltd, 11 Welbeck Street, London W1.
  Fixed roofs and rising roofs. Land Rover and Range Rover.
Cavalier Coachmen, Walton Avenue, Felixstowe, Suffolk.
  Cruise vans—fixed roofs and high tops. Bedford, Fiat, Ford,
  Mercedes, Renault, Sherpa, Toyota, VW, VW LT.
Compass Caravans Ltd, Riverside Industrial Estate, Langley
  Park, Durham.
  Coachbuilts. Bedford, Mercedes.
Dethleffs Caravans UK, PO Box 29, Halifax, West Yorks.
  A-class coachbuilts from Germany. Mercedes.
Devon Conversions Ltd, Vulcan Works, Water Lane, Exeter,
  Devon.
  Rising roofs and high tops. Mercedes, Toyota, VW.
Foster and Day, 1050 Manchester Road, Castleton, Rochdale,
  Lancs.
  Coachbuilts. Bedford, Ford, Sherpa.
Glendale Motor Homes, Unit 3, Wincolmlec, Hull, North
  Humberside.
  Bedford, Ford, Mazda, Peugeot, Talbot, Toyota.
GT Motorised Ltd, Riverside Works, Grovehill Road, Beverley,
  Humberside.
  Coachbuilts. Bedford, Fiat Daily, Renault, Talbot.

Richard Holdsworth Conversions Ltd, Headley Road East, Woodley, Reading, Berks.
Rising roofs, high tops and coachbuilts. Bedford, Ford, Renault, VW.

Island Plastics, Edward Street, Ryde, Isle of Wight.
Dismountables for small trucks and hatchback cars. Daihatsu, Honda, Suzuki, hatchback cars.

Madisons, Blackpool Road, Clifton, Preston, Lancs.
A-class coachbuilts from Germany. Mercedes, Peugeot.

Motorhomes International, 345 High Street, Berkhamsted, Herts.
Rising roofs, high tops and A-class coachbuilts from Germany. Colt, Datsun, Fiat, Mercedes, Renault, Suzuki, Toyota, VW.

Nomadic Wheels, Coombe Park Business and Leisure Vehicle Centre, Ashprington, Totnes, S. Devon.
Fixed roof multi-purpose conversions. Bedford, Fiat Ducato.

Pampas Motor Caravans Ltd, Gresham Road, Derby.
Rising roofs and high tops. Ford, VW LT.

Pioneer Recreational Vehicles Ltd, 147–157 Somerset Street, Hessle Road, Hull, North Humberside.
Coachbuilts: Bedford, Colt, Fiat Daily, Mercedes.

Travelworld Motorhomes, The Leisure Mall, Fordhouses, Wolverhampton.
Chevrolet, Mercedes, VW.

B. Walker & Son Ltd, Gammons Lane, Watford, Herts.
Dismountables and cruise vans. Bedford, Colt, Ford, Land Rover, Renault, Sherpa, Talbot, Toyota, VW.

Who makes what?

CB = coachbuilt   CBA = A-class coachbuilt   DM = dismountable
FR = fixed low roof   HT = fixed high top   RR = rising roof

Altus	HT	VW LT	Cavalier Coachmen
Amigo	RR	Fiat 900	Motorhomes International
Apache	CB	VW LT	Auto-Trail
Bravo	RR	Mitsubishi Colt	Motorhomes International
Caravelle	RR	Fiat 900	Motorhomes International
Caribbean	HT	Fiat Daily	Cavalier Coachmen
Cherokee	RR	Datsun	Motorhomes International
Cheyenne	CB	Peugeot 504	Auto-Trail
Cirrus	FR	Bedford	Cavalier Coachmen
Classic	HT	VW	Cavalier Coachmen
Clipper	CB	Bedford, Mercedes	Compass Caravans

Club	HT	VW	Cavalier Coachmen
Comanche	CB	Bedford	Auto-Trail
Continental	RR	Land Rover	Carawagon
Cumulus	FR HT	Bedford	Cavalier Coachmen
Custom	FR	Bedford	Nomadic Wheels
Dethleffs	CBA	Mercedes	from Godfrey Davis
Diamond	HT RR	Mercedes, VW	Travelworld
Discovery	HT	Mercedes	Devon Conversions
Double Top	RR	Toyota	Devon Conversions
Drifter	CB	Bedford	Compass Caravans
Excalibur	CB	Talbot Express.	Autohomes (UK)
Executive	FR	Bedford, Fiat Iveco	Nomadic Wheels
Globetrotter	CBA	Mercedes	Dethleffs
Hi-Flyer	HT	Ford, Renault, VW	Richard Holdsworth
Hitch Hiker	DM	Hatchback car	Island Plastics
Horizon	CB	Bedford, Ford, Sherpa	Foster and Day
Huntsman	HT	VW	Motorhomes International
Hymer-Mobil	CBA	Mercedes	from Motorhomes International
Kamper	RR	VW	Autohomes (UK)
Laredo	HT	VW LT	Pampas Motor Caravans
Leader	RR	Renault	Motorhomes International
Legend	CB	Chevrolet	Travelworld
Leisure	RR	Sherpa	Auto-Sleepers
Mayflower	RR HT	Mercedes	Devon Conversions
Meteor	FR	Fiat Ducato	Nomadic Wheels
Miami	CB	Fiat Daily	GT Motorised
Mini-Motorhome	CB	Pickup trucks	Glendale
Mondo	FR	Bedford	Nomadic Wheels
Moonraker	FR RR	VW	Devon Conversions
Motorhome	CB	Bedford, Ford	Autohomes (UK)
Motorsleeper	HT	VW	Motorhomes International
Murvi	FR	Bedford, Fiat Iveco	Nomadic Wheels
Nevada	RR	VW LT	Pampas Motor Caravans
Orlando	CB	Bedford	GT Motorised
Pandora	RR	Fiat 900	Autohomes (UK)
Pompano	CB	Bedford	GT Motorised
Ranger	CB	Bedford, Ford, Sherpa	Richard Holdsworth
Rio-Grande	RR	Toyota	Motorhomes International
Romahome	DM	Daihatsu, Honda, Suzuki	Island Plastics
Romance	RR HT	Renault	Richard Holdsworth

Safari	FR	Land Rover	Carawagon
Savannah	RR	Bedford, Ford	Canterbury Conversions
Stratus	FR HT	Bedford	Cavalier Coachmen
Sultan	RR	Sherpa	Richard Holdsworth
Sundancer	HT	Fiat Ducato	Motorhomes International
Sunhome	HT	Bedford, Ford	Canterbury Conversions
Sunrise	RR	VW	Devon Conversions
Suntrekker	DM	Flatbed or pickup	B. Walker & Son
Tabbert	CBA	Mercedes	from Madisons
Tampa	CB	Bedford	GT Motorised
Texan	HT	Ford	Pampas Motor Caravans
Trailblazer	RR	Bedford, Ford	Autohomes (UK)
Travelhome	CB	Bedford, Ford	Autohomes (UK)
Tri-Star	RR	Suzuki	Motorhomes International
Utopian	RR	Bedford	Auto-Sleepers
Villa	FR RR HT	VW	Richard Holdsworth
Vogue	CBA	Chevrolet	Travelworld
Weekender	DM	Hatchback car	Island Plastics
Xplorer	RR	VW	Motorhomes International

Appendix 3
Some useful addresses

These lists are merely representative. Consult telephone directories or specialist magazines for further addresses.

Modifications, repairs, 'specials' to order

AB Services, Stoke Plain Lodge, Stoke Bruerne, Towcester, Northants.
Conversions.

Bedford Coachworks Co Ltd, Church Road, Wilsted, Beds.
Coachbuilts.

Bowers Motorcaravans, Green Lawns Service Station, Luton Road, Harpenden, Herts.
Modifications and repairs.

Brownhills Ltd, Fosseway, Elston, Newark, Notts.
'Suntor' conversion of Morris Ital van.

Car Camper Sales Co, 2 Springfields, Prixford, Barnstaple, Devon.
Conversions—mainly large.

Cavalier Coachmen, Walton Avenue, Felixstowe, Suffolk.
Modifications and refurbishing.

Challenger Motor Bodies, Highfield House, Keelby Road, Little London, Grimsby.
Dismountables.

Corvesgate Coachcraft, Unit 17, Elliott Road, West Howe, Bournemouth, Dorset.
Coachbuilts and modifications.

Godfrey Davis Caravans, High Street, Epping, Essex.
Modifications and repairs.

Richard Holdsworth Conversions Ltd, Headley Road East, Woodley, Reading, Berks.
Conversions.

Jennings Coachwork Ltd, Second Avenue, Weston Road, Crewe, Cheshire.
Conversions and coachbuilts.

Manchester Motor Caravan Co, 30 Frederick Road, Salford, Manchester.
Conversions and coachbuilts.

Penta Motorhomes, Box Road, Bath, Avon.
  Repairs.
Southern Cross Campers, Pantiles Park, London Road, Bagshot, Surrey.
  Repairs and refurbishing.
TMA, 8–22 Athol Road, Walsgrave, Coventry.
  Custom vans.
Watling, 88 Parkstreet Village, St Albans, Herts.
  Towing brackets, including specials.

Roofs, windows, furniture kits

Birmingham Motor Caravans, Victoria Street, Small Heath, Birmingham.
Bristol Coachbuilders, Frenchay Park Service Station, Frenchay, Bristol.
S. W. Brown & Co, Rushey Lane, Tyseley, Birmingham. (Sheldon roofs)
G. A. Cooper, The Vehicle Window Centre, 10 Crawshaw Close, Pudsey, Leeds, W. Yorks. (windows)
DIY Motor Caravan Centre, 230 High Street, Harlesden, London NW10.
Richard Holdsworth Conversions Ltd, (address above)
Invincible Motor Caravans, 29 High Road, Balham, London SW12.
Manchester Motor Caravan Co (address above)
RGA Conversions, West End, Old Costessey, Norwich.
Spacemaker Systems, High Street, Berkhamsted, Herts. (roofs)

Wholesalers of accessories and equipment

H. Burden Ltd, Pytchley Lodge Road Industrial Estate, Kettering, Northants.
Joy & King Ltd, 15 Alperton Lane, Perivale, Greenford, Middx.
ET Riddiough Sales Ltd, Victoria Works, Barrowford, Nelson, Lancs.
  Catalogues available; supplies from local agents.

Clubs

Auto Camping Club, 5 Dunsfold Rise, Coulsdon, Surrey CR3 2ED. For all types of camping units.

Camping & Caravanning Club (Camping Club of Great Britain & Ireland), 11 Lower Grosvenor Place, London SW1W 0EY. Separate motorcaravan section.

Caravan Club, East Grinstead House, East Grinstead, W. Sussex RH19 1UA. For trailers and motorcaravans.

Motor Caravanners' Club, 52 Wolseley Road, London N8 8RP. Especially for motorcaravans.

All clubs offer lists of sites at home and abroad, magazines or newsletters, insurance and social activities. All have regional groups. Caravan Club is largest with 250,000 full members. ACC and MCC are comparatively small.

Magazines

Motorcaravan + Motorhome Monthly, Sanglier Press Services Ltd, 104 St Lukes Road, Old Windsor, Berks.

Motor Caravan World, Stone Industrial Publications Ltd, Andrew House, 2A Granville Road, Sidcup, Kent DA14 4BN.

Camping, caravanning and motoring magazines report on motorcaravans occasionally.

Books

Brooks, Bill. *All about Motor Caravanning* (Pitman, 1975).

Brooks, Bill. *Motorists' Guide to Motor Caravanning* (RAC, 1979).

Hewat, Theresa and Jonathan. *Overland and Beyond* (Roger Lascelles, revised ed, 1981).

Lockwood, Tim. *Recreational Vehicle Maintenance* (Selpress, 1973).

Lyons, Stanley. *Motor Caravanning at Home and Abroad* (Yeoman, 1973).

Myhill, Henry. *Motor Caravanning—a Complete Guide* (Ward Lock, 1976).

Park, Chris. *Drive it! The Complete Book of Motor-Caravanning* (Haynes, 1979).

Prendergast, John. *The Road to India* (John Murray, 1977).

Sworder, John. *Free to Roam* (EP Publishing, 1983).

Many caravanning books have chapters about motorcaravans.

Miscellaneous

Aqua-Marine Mfg (UK) Ltd, 216 Fair Oak Road, Bishopstoke, Eastleigh, Hants SO5 6NJ. 12V compressor refrigerator.

G. F. Barron, Court Barton, Newton St Cyres, Exeter, Devon.
Hot water tanks using engine heat.

CAK Ltd, 10 Princes Drive, Kenilworth, Warks.
Water and waste tanks.

Canvas Holidays, Bull Plain, Hertford SG14 1DY.
Sited tents.

Consumers' Association, 14 Buckingham Street, London WC2N
6DS.
Publishers of *Which?*

Danfoss Ltd, Perivale Industrial Estate, Horsenden Lane South,
Greenford, Middlesex UB6 7QE.
Parts for making 12V compressor refrigerator.

Deneway Guides and Travel, PO Box 286, Rottingdean, Brigh-
ton, Sussex BN2 8AY.
Alan Rogers's critical sites guides.

Eberspächer (UK) Ltd, Fibbards Road, Brockenhurst, Hants SO4
7RD.
Petrol or diesel interior heater.

Electrolux Ltd, Leisure Products Division, Luton, Beds LU4
9QQ.
Peltier type cool/hot box. Refrigerators.

Eurocamp Travel Ltd, Edmundson House, Tatton Street, Knuts-
ford, Cheshire WA16 1BG.
Sited tents and caravans.

Freshfields Holidays, 93 Newman Street, London W1P 3LE.
Sited tents and caravans.

Kennford International Caravan Park, Kennford, Exeter, Devon
EX6 7YN.
List of 'Best of British' caravan sites.

Leisure Accessories Ltd, 6 Guardian Road Industrial Estate,
Norwich NR5 8PR.
'Qest' plumbing system.

Selpress Books, 35 High Street, Wendover, Bucks.
American maintenance manuals.

Wilcomatic Group, 512 Purley Way, Croydon, Surrey CR9 4LR.
Peltier type cool/hot box.

Wotec Leisure Products, 18 Church View, Carterton, Oxford.
Hot water tanks using engine heat.

Index

Figures in italics indicate illustrations